Fit, Function and Flourish

Your Place and Function in the Local Church

Tom Peers

Fit, Function and Flourish
Your Place and Function in the Local Church

Ragamuffin Publishing Company - Portland, Maine
www.ragamuffinpublishing.com
tom@ragamuffinpublishing.com

Fit, Function and Flourish/ Tom Peers - 2nd edition

ISBN 13: 978-0-9970998-2-9

* For emphasis—bold or underlining within quotes are not part of the original quote.

Contents

Preface

This is the second edition of *Fit, Function and Flourish.* It was originally published thirty years ago, in 1987. At that time, five thousand copies were printed, and when they were gone, that was it, the book was never reprinted. It's only lately (January 2017), that I felt the urge to update, expand and reprint it, and for one main reason—it still addresses an important topic touching on relevant issues for the believer and local church.

This edition will include some things I've learned in the thirty years that have elapsed. I believe what's said in this book is even more relevant today than thirty years ago. Why? Because today there is a marked increase of decrease. Say what? There is a marked and noticeable increase in the number of Christians who have joined the ranks of the unchurched. I'm hearing now that core believers in churches who previously attended weekly, are now attending once every three or four weeks. Non-core attenders may attend once every couple months, if that.

In my opinion, this points to the reality of what was prophesied in 1 Timothy 4.

1 Timothy 4:1

> Now the Spirit expressly says that in later times some will depart from the faith.

You can't depart from something you weren't first part of! There's no doubt in my mind that this is happening right now, indicating that we're in the very end of the end times. If we combine that with another sign of the end times that Jesus Himself taught about in Matthew 12, I think all doubt can safely be removed.

Matthew 24:12

> Sin will be rampant everywhere, and the love of many will grow cold. (NLT)

That statement isn't just true for unbelievers, unfortunately it's true for believers as well. Many people's love for God, the things of God, the presence of God, for evangelism and for the local church have grown cold. But it doesn't have to be that way, and that's why this book is important. Paul admonished us to stir up the passions and gifts that are inside of us.

2 Timothy 1:6

> For this reason I remind you to fan into flame the gift of God, which is in you.

"Fan into flame" indicates that gifts and passions have grown cold through neglect and disuse. It's time for those who count themselves serious about the Lordship of Jesus Christ and spiritual growth to stir up and fan into flame those passions and gifts that are to be used for kingdom business. It's time Christians learn to *fit* and *function* so that both they and their local churches can *flourish.*

Introduction

I was called by God as a pastor-teacher to help people connect with God through Jesus Christ, and then grow spiritually. That calling is the starting point of this book. In my God-ordained mission of helping people grow spiritually, I've noticed through the years some people I just couldn't help. Seeing these people not growing or thriving began to pique my interest, and I prayed about why this was.

One night when sound asleep, the Spirit of God woke me up. This by itself is a miracle because rarely am I awakened by anyone or anything. The Holy Spirit distinctly said within my spirit four words, "Fit, Function, and Flourish." I know that sounds spooky and super-spiritual to some people, but to be clear, this is the only time in my life that I heard the voice of the Lord that strong. I have sensed the voice of God many times in direct but gentle ways, but this night it was definitive and strong.

That was all that the Lord said to me, "Fit, function and flourish." I leaned over, turned on the light, grabbed a pad and pen, and wrote the words down, knowing that I might lose them if I didn't.

As I laid back down, I meditated on those words...*fit, function, and flourish.* Like a flash, revelation came, illuminating what God was saying to me. I knew exactly what the Lord meant by those words. The next day, I wrote out the message behind the four words and, shortly afterwards, preached it as a series of messages in the church I pastored at the time in Rochester, New York.

Not long after this experience, the Holy Spirit told me to preach this message at most of the churches where I was invited to speak. Sometime later, I felt impressed of the Lord to put the message in writing, in book form. My initial reaction to writing a book was negative. It wasn't that I didn't want the message to go out. My inner conflict was over the motivation of publishing a book. Was it really the Lord, or just ego? After careful examination of my heart, I was sure that it wasn't ego or self-aggrandizement, but truly a leading from God. My motive was and is to help the Body of Christ as a whole, and individuals in particular.

As I said earlier, the content of this book came from the Spirit of God in a flash, not from untold hours of diligent study. I saw what was missing in many Christian's lives, something that hindered their spiritual growth or God's blessing on their lives. Since beginning to preach and teach this message, I have seen numerous people apply this teaching with significant results in their walk with God.

I know that if you will read this book thoroughly (not while watching TV or checking your smart phone for the millionth time today) and with an open mind, you'll discover a biblical principle that will affect your life in a significant way.

There are conditions to God's promises and blessings. Some people scoff at that, but Scripture confirms this truth over and over. Here's just one example.

John 15:7

If you abide in me, and my words abide in you, ask whatever you wish, and it will be done for you.

But, what if a person doesn't abide in Christ, can they expect their prayers to be answered? What if God's Word doesn't abide in them, can they expect their prayers to be answered? Not if Jesus' words mean anything! Clearly here, there is a condition to the promise of answered prayer. We poo-poo this to our own detriment.

Similarly, there are a several conditions we see in God's Word that need to be met in order to experience God's blessings. Faithful giving of tithes and offerings with a cheerful heart is one key that opens God's blessings to the believer (Malachi 3:10). Praying in faith, not doubting, is a key (James 1:6). Not willfully and intentionally living in sin is another (Psalm 66:18). But the people I knew who weren't thriving in life or growing spiritually were doing those things. I knew there had to be something else involved.

The principles in this book are meant to work in conjunction with other biblical principles that deal with Christians thriving in life. Please don't interpret this book as saying that the only thing needed to succeed in life is to fit and function in a local church. We all know there is more to it than that. Yet, this idea of fitting and functioning is a critical piece in our journey with God. We ignore it to our own peril.

I also would like to go on record as saying that I am not advocating a "hyper-church" philosophy. I realize that the local church and where it fits into God's plan for individual believers, is only one part of the entire picture. What I AM saying is that the principles in this book are essential to successful spiritual growth and that these principles need to be looked at carefully and applied in harmony with all other biblical principles.

The concept of people fitting and functioning in the Body of Christ particularly needs voicing at this time in church history. Any pastor will tell you that the committed core who are engaged in accomplishing the church's vision is small and appears to be getting smaller.

Once I heard a story of a group of ants who were plotting a way to get revenge on a certain elephant. The elephant would come down the jungle path and devastate nearby ant hills with its trunk. So one day the ants got up on a tree limb hanging over the elephant's path. When the elephant came down the path and under the tree, thousands of ants jumped off the limb and onto the elephant's back. The elephant, with one massive swing of its trunk, sent all the ants flying into the air—all, that is, except for one lone ant who was hanging onto the elephant's neck. All of the ants who had been flung off looked up and began to shout up to the lone ant, "Choke him to death! Come on, choke him!"

That is exactly what has happened in most churches. In most cases, there is a multitude sitting around the 15-20% diligent few saying, "Come on, you can do it, you can expand God's kingdom here on the earth and topple Satan's kingdom, come on, choke him to death!" Folks, it just doesn't work that way. Establishing the kingdom of God and toppling Satan's work in your community takes everyone. Even a cursory reading of Acts 2:42-47 would show this.

There are two extremes or ditches in everything: neglect and overemphasis. In this book, I don't want to be guilty of the latter. If it seems that way, it's only because there's been neglect in the Body of Christ concerning the biblical principles of the believer's place in the local church. My prayer is that the Holy Spirit will use this book to further His kingdom and bring Him glory. Amen.

CHAPTER 1

Appointed to Flourish

One of the most important things you as a New Testament believer must establish is whether it's God's will for you to flourish and thrive in this life? Without this question being answered firmly in your mind, you will be misled or in a state of confusion for the rest of your life. There is a principle in the Word which simply says, "Faith begins where the will of God is known." You cannot go beyond your knowledge of the Word of God in any given area. You can't pray in faith for something you're not sure is God's will in the first place. Our first chapter, therefore, will deal solely with this issue: Are we appointed by God to flourish or not?

The word *flourish* means, "to grow vigorously, succeed, thrive, be productive and have influence." Are those things God's will as revealed in Scripture? Let's find out.

Joshua 1:8

> This Book of the Law shall not depart from your mouth, but you shall meditate on it day and night, so that you may be careful to do according to all that is written in it. For then you will **make your way prosperous, and then you will have good success.**

The verse says that if we speak, think, and do the Word of God, we'll be prosperous and succeed. Why do people want to debate this, as if God really didn't mean it? You would think that people would be thrilled to hear that God wants them to succeed, prosper and thrive in this life.

3 John 2

> Beloved, I pray **that all may go well with you** and that you may **be in good health**, as it goes well with your soul.

When you're spiritually, emotionally and physically healthy, and things are going well with you…you're flourishing!

Our lives here on Planet Earth touch or experience life in eight basic realms:

1. **Spiritual**
   Relationship with God and His body— the church.

2. **Physical**
   Health of your physical body.

3. **Emotional**

Mature, right-thinking and reacting. Self-control. The experience of love, peace and joy.

4. **Intellectual**
   Continual learning, engaged in activities that stretch our minds as we grow in the knowledge of our world.

5. **Career**
   Success in your career and occupation.

6. **Financial/Material**
   Financial and material provision, abundance.

7. **Relational**
   Healthy relationships with spouse, children, family, friends and coworkers.

8. **Social**
   Healthy and positive contribution to your community and world.

3 John 2 says that just as God wants it to go well with your soul, He also wants it to go well in other areas of your life. Can anyone adequately make the case that God wants us to thrive spiritually but not in these other areas? I don't believe they can.

How about the financial and material realm?

Philippians 4:19

> And my God will supply every need of yours according to his riches in glory in Christ Jesus.

If every material need is supplied, you're thriving!

2 Corinthians 9:8

And God is able to make **all** grace abound to you, so that having **all** sufficiency in **all** things at **all** times, you may abound in **every** good work.

The subject of that chapter is financial and material, and notice the adjectives—"**all** grace, **all** sufficiency in **all** things at **all** times, in **every** good work"—that's thriving, that's flourishing.

How about health? We already read in 3 John 2 that God wants us to be in good health even as it goes well our souls. God is for our health and healing.

Deuteronomy 7:15

And the Lord will take away from you all sickness

Psalm 103:2-3

Bless the Lord, O my soul, and forget not all his benefits, who forgives all your iniquity, **who heals all your diseases**.

Would it make any sense for God to say, "I want you to thrive in only two or three of the eight areas of life"? God's will is that you flourish, thrive and live in abundance in every area.

Psalm 66:12

We went through fire and through water; yet you have brought us out to a place of abundance.

The Hebrew word for *abundance* here is *revayah*, which means a place of flourishing or saturated abundance. The picture being drawn here is that of a fruit tree so loaded down with fruit that its branches are bowed down. That's abundance! It's the very same Hebrew word as *runneth over* in Psalm 23:5...*my cup* ***runneth over*** (KJV).

God has appointed you to flourish in **whatever you do.**

Psalm 1:3

> He (the person who delights and meditates on the Word of God) is like a tree planted by streams of water that yields its fruit in its season, and its leaf does not wither. **In all that he does, he prospers.**

Deuteronomy 29:9

> Therefore keep the words of this covenant and do them, **that you may prosper in all that you do.**

And God has appointed you to flourish **wherever you go.**

Joshua 1:7

> Only be strong and very courageous, being careful to do according to all the law that Moses my servant commanded you. Do not turn from it to the right hand or to the left, **that you may have good success wherever you go.**

When I teach on flourishing, thriving and success, even financial success, I say that God wants us to live in that place of abundance, that place of *revayah*, for four main reasons.

Four Main Reasons for Abundance

1. To sow into and finance the gospel into the world.
   Deuteronomy 8:18

You shall remember the Lord your God, for it is he who gives you power to get wealth**, that he may confirm his covenant** that he swore to your fathers, as it is this day.

2. To give to those in need.
   2 Corinthians 9:11

You will be enriched in every way **to be generous in every way**.

3. To care and provide well for our families.
   1 Timothy 5:8

But if anyone does not provide for his relatives, and especially for members of his household, he has denied the faith and is worse than an unbeliever.

4. To enjoy life.
   1 Timothy 6:17

God, who richly provides us with everything to enjoy.

One time I was teaching and I drew three horizontal lines, one on top of the other. I said that the middle line is just barely getting your needs met, nothing more, nothing less. The top line is abundance, more than your bare minimum needs. And the bottom line is your needs not being met, the place of deficiency. Then I asked a rhetorical question, "Which line represents God's will for His children?"

1. Abundance ______________

2. Needs being met __________

3. Needs NOT being met _______

Most said the middle line, just barely having your needs met. I then asked, "So how can you possibly sow significant finances into your church, parachurch ministries and world missions if you don't have extra to give? How can you give to those in need if you don't have extra to give? How can you provide to your family a decent living and lifestyle, if you don't have anything to eat other than bread and water or Ramen Noodles (nothing against Ramen Noodles, I like them)? How can you enjoy a vacation and have some fun things to do with your family if you don't have extra? After that, I taught on what God's Word teaches about these things.

I'm always amazed at people who will fight you for the right to fail in life and always be under, not over. I don't believe that represents God's will. If we put God first, He wants to bless us above the 'barely needs met' line.

Deuteronomy 28:13

> The Lord will make you the head and not the tail, and you **only will be above**, and you will **not be underneath**, if you listen to the commandments of the Lord your God. (NASB)

Matthew 6:33

> But seek first the kingdom of God and his righteousness, and all these things will be **added to you.**

God adds to you, not subtracts. And this is true for all eight realms we experience in life. God wants us to flourish. Period.

By way of clarification...this does NOT mean we should equate poverty with a lack of being close to God or wealth as a sign of spirituality. I don't mean that at all. But I am saying that it's God's will for us to flourish in all eight realms of life. The only exception I can see to this is adversity and suffering which is caused by persecution. An example would be the Apostle Paul who experienced adversity and lack because of persecution for the name of Christ. I believe that suffering persecution is the only kind we're NOT redeemed from. Barring that, God's will is for us to flourish, thrive and have success in all areas of life.

CHAPTER 2

Flourishing: The Result of Growth

God has given this generation more knowledge of His Word than any previous generation in the history of the world. There have been numerous times down through the ages that certain individuals, such as Martin Luther, have received enlightenment on a particular truth that changed the trajectory of Christendom. In Martin Luther's case, it was the revelation that *the just shall live by faith* (Rom. 1:17). But much of the time these truths remained only with these men or women and their loyal followers, and didn't spread quickly to the masses of other believers.

Today, it's very different. There has been a literal explosion of knowledge of the Word of God, an explosion that gets more intense every day. Yes, we still have men and women who have spearheaded this explosion, but never before have so many people known so much about victorious Christian living through the Word of God. This explosion of knowledge (both secular and biblical) is a fulfillment of biblical prophecy.

Daniel 12:4

But you, Daniel, shut up the words and seal the book, until the time of the end. **Many shall run to and fro**, and **knowledge shall increase.**

From this verse, there are two things that will happen at "the time of the end," in other words, the end of time as we know it.

1. ***Many will run to and fro.*** This means there will be a dramatic increase in world travel, both in distance and speed. And it says in the end time "many" will be experiencing this kind of travel. The twentieth century saw this fulfilled, and in the twenty-first century it's even more pronounced.

2. ***Knowledge will increase.*** The end time will also be marked with a dramatic increase in knowledge, and that means knowledge in all areas. We can't even begin to fathom the increase in knowledge in the twentieth and twenty-first centuries in the areas of medicine, physics, biology, cosmology, electricity, space, aviation, transportation, communication, mathematics, industry and technology. It just boggles the mind.

One area of that has significantly increased is the knowledge and distribution of God's Word.

Matthew 24:14

This gospel of the kingdom will be proclaimed throughout the whole world as a testimony to all nations, and then the end will come.

With the advent of radio, TV, satellite communication and the Internet, the knowledge and distribution of God's Word to the world has increased exponentially. Additionally, knowledge that was only accessible to pastors, ministers and seminarians, is now easily available to your average Christian. One can instantly access a commentary, translation, theology book or Greek definition on their smart phone while waiting for their doctor's appointment!

One problem resulting from this explosion of knowledge of God's Word is that our experience is lagging far behind our knowledge. Many Christians have grown spiritually fat and lazy. There is a tendency to view knowledge as an end in and of itself; but, in actuality, knowledge is the means to an end. God wants us to take that knowledge and put it to work, to apply it so we can bear fruit.

There are four main phases of the intake of truth.

1. **Information** (reading God's Word).
2. **Meditation** (studying and pondering God's Word).
3. **Revelation** (understanding and enlightenment as to what God's Word means).
4. **Application** (acting on God's Word, putting it into practice).

It seems we have majored on the first three phases at the expense of the fourth!

Many people pride themselves on their vast reservoir of knowledge but are found wanting when it comes to applying what they have learned. The focus should be the application, not just the information. Paul touched on this in Philippians 4.

Philippians 4:9

> What you have learned and received and heard and seen in me—**practice these things**, and the God of peace will be with you.

The peace of God is with those who practice the Word of God, not with those who just sit in a chair and hear the God's Word. Many people have enough of God's Word in them to blow the devil out of this universe, but their focus should be toward this fourth element—application.

You Flourish When You Grow

It's not enough to know that it's God's will for you to flourish. I want to teach you how to flourish as a believer. God hasn't left us in the dark about this. He has given us some very important conditions to be met that precede flourishing. It's only when we align ourselves with these biblical principles that we'll experience the fullest measure of success. Psalm 92 gives important insight into the "how" of flourishing.

Psalm 92:12

> The righteous **flourish** like the palm tree and **grow** like a cedar in Lebanon.

Notice the connection between the concept of *flourishing* and *growth*. They are closely related.

One of the definitions of *flourish* is "to grow luxuriantly or thrive." This shows how close the relationship is between these two components. The relationship is simple: **You flourish only when you grow.** We could put it another way: Growth results in flourishing. This is true in the natural as well as the spiritual. If someone's growth, either physically or emotionally, has been stunted for some reason, that person will not flourish or prosper to the same degree had full growth occurred.

The word *flourish* could also mean "to bear fruit, to yield and produce fruit." We see this in verse 14.

Psalm 92:14

> They (the ones who flourish) still bear fruit in old age; they are ever full of sap and green ("spiritual vitality" -Amplified Bible Classic Edition).

So we have two components working here; *growth*, which produces *flourishing*. But these two ideas are connected to a third element, and that is found in the verse between verses 12 and 14.

Psalm 92:13

They are **planted** in the house of the Lord; they **flourish** in the courts of our God.

Growing and flourishing are connected to being ***planted** in the house of the Lord* and flourishing there.

In the Old Testament, the house of the Lord was the temple, but in the New Testament, this is a picture of both the individual believer and the church.

1 Corinthians 3:16

Do you not know that you are God's temple and that God's Spirit dwells in you?

This verse is talking about the church there in Corinth. This is NOT talking about the believer's physical body...that verse comes three chapters later (1 Corinthians 6:19 - Or do you not know that your body is a temple of the Holy Spirit within you, whom you have from God?). But 1 Corinthians 3:16 is talking about the local church. The Amplified Bible says, *Do you not know and understand that you [the church] are the temple of God, and that the Spirit of God dwells [permanently] in you [collectively and individually]?*

The idea here is that **flourishing**, **growth** and being **planted** in the house of the Lord are all talked about together and are all interrelated.

Flourishing is dependent upon growing, and growing is dependent upon being planted in the house of the Lord (we'll apply that to the local church) and bearing fruit there! Many people want to flourish, but they don't want to grow. Many people want to flourish in life, but they don't want to be planted in the house of the Lord, the church. Many people want to thrive spiritually, but they refuse to obey certain conditions that precede flourishing. But God's Word says these things are all tied in with each other.

Planted does not mean roaming from church to church. The word *planted* means to "put down roots." It means to stay some place and grow deep roots there. Many Christians float from church to church and then wonder why they are not prospering or flourishing in their own individual lives. It's not a mystery at all. You can't yield fruit until you are planted and put down roots.

If you plant an apple tree, and then jerk it out of the ground two weeks later, do you honestly think it's going to grow and produce fruit? Of course not! Yet, that is exactly what many Christians have been doing with their individual walks with God. They attend a particular church, but when the pastor says or does something they don't like, they become offended and leave. Then they begin attending another church and, when they hear or see something there that they don't like, they leave that church as well. On and on it goes, all their lives, never having put down roots in the New Covenant "house of the Lord."

To grow healthy and strong, you need a consistent, healthy diet. Many church floaters, however, are just after junk food and snacks, their favorite line of teaching. About the time God is endeavoring to get through to them with a different diet, they leave and go to another church after more junk food. You need a proper diet to grow healthy. Don't leave a church because the pastor is switching from French fries (the blessings, answered prayer, victory, overcoming, the book of Revelation) to spinach (holiness, prayer, service, commitment, tithing).

One definition of *flourish* means *to bear fruit.* Question: When is the best time to eat fruit? The answer is...when it's ripe or mature. When is the best time believers flourish and bear fruit? When they mature and grow. God's will is for you to get planted, grow and then yield fruit.

Psalm 1:2-3

> His (the believer's) delight is in the law of the Lord, and on his law he meditates day and night. He is like a tree planted by streams of water that yields its fruit in its season, and its leaf does not wither. In all that he does, he prospers.

Again, we see a connection between being planted and yielding fruit or thriving. We see this same principle in Colossians.

Colossians 1:9-10

> And so, from the day we heard, we have not ceased to pray for you, asking that you may be **filled with the knowledge** of his will in all **spiritual wisdom and understanding**, so as to walk in a manner worthy of the Lord, fully pleasing to him: **bearing fruit** in every good work and **increasing in the knowledge** (speaks of maturity) of God;

Notice that knowledge, wisdom and understanding come first—and those things causing you to bear fruit in every good work. Both the New American Standard Bible and the New International Version begin verse 10 with the words, "so that," which means "resulting in." What is this verse saying? It's saying that verse 10 (bearing fruit) is a direct result of verse 9 (being filled with knowledge, wisdom and understanding). Knowledge, wisdom and understanding come first, then comes the yielding of fruit (flourishing).

The word *wisdom* itself is a word that speaks to us of maturity and growth. Paul said in 1 Corinthians 2:6, *Yet we do speak wisdom among those who are mature (NASB).* Wisdom is connected to maturity and growth. So we have in Colossians 1 exactly what was said in Psalm 92—that you will flourish (bear fruit) only after you grow and mature.

As I said earlier in this chapter, many people have a lot of knowledge, but that does not mean they have grown up. There is a vast difference between having knowledge and growing up. Knowledge by itself won't help you a bit. Sometimes it actually can become a liability. Paul said in 1 Corinthians 8:1, *Knowledge makes arrogant (NASB).* The NIV says, *Knowledge puffs up.* Have you ever known someone who used any and every opportunity to spew out their knowledge, even if it was never asked for? They use every chance they get to unleash their knowledge on you. Did you ever also notice that many of these same people never want to roll up their sleeves and get involved with anything? They can give you advice on lots of things; but, when it comes to work, forget it, they're not interested. Knowledge by itself is useless except when combined with application.

Remember, flourishing is a result of growth, and growth is connected to being planted in the house of the Lord, which we're applying to the local church (1 Corinthians 3:16). We'll be referring to these Biblical concepts throughout the remainder of the book, so it's important that you understand them now. You must come to realize that flourishing won't come to the fullest extent until you are obedient to God in the area of being "planted" somewhere. A certain amount of growth can occur without being planted in a local church, but it's for the most part short-lived and superficial, and certainly exists without a key aspect of growth, accountability.

You can stay home on Sunday mornings and watch your favorite TV pastor, but that will not produce lasting growth or stability. Flourishing comes from growth when you are firmly planted and have put down roots into a good local church. That Sunday morning TV or Internet pastor doesn't know you and can't shepherd you the way God wants you to be shepherded (pastored). He or she can't monitor your progress, or the lack of it, as a pastor or church leader in a local church can. That pastor or church leader can get into your life to some degree and help you with areas that need attention (which, by the way, is why some people don't go to church!). He or she can also help channel your gifts, talents and passions where they are best suited. Keep reading because you will see this truth more clearly as we continue.

CHAPTER 3

Components of Growth

If flourishing is dependent upon maturity and growth, it would do us well to take a closer look at the subject of growth to determine how it occurs. First, you must realize that spiritual growth is not an option, it's a command.

Hebrews 6:1

> Therefore let us leave the elementary doctrine of Christ and go on to maturity.

The Amplified Bible puts it this way:

> Therefore let us get past the elementary stage in the teachings about the Christ, advancing on to maturity and perfection and spiritual completeness.

Advancing on to maturity is a command that must be obeyed as would any other command from God IF we take the Lordship of Jesus Christ seriously.

Jesus commanded us in Matthew 28:19 to make disciples of all nations. Notice that Jesus said to make *disciples*, not *converts*. There is a big difference between a disciple and a convert. Converts are babies in Christ and haven't grown spiritually yet. Disciples grow up and become diligent followers of Christ. It's fine to be a convert initially for a time, but the Lord expects ongoing spiritual growth to become a committed disciple. A "disciple" is one who continues.

John 8:31

> So Jesus was saying to those Jews who had believed Him, "If you **continue** in My word, then you are truly disciples of Mine." (NASB)

There are two main components that must exist before any real growth can occur. One component without the other won't work. It's only when we have both components in balance that we experience genuine growth. If we were to put these components into an equation, it would look like this:

Nourishment + Exercise = Growth

This equation is true for the spiritual as well as the natural. It doesn't matter whether you have been saved for two days or twenty years, this formula is valid for everyone. When it comes to the believer's spiritual growth related to the local church, the nourishment part of our equation is regular attendance, for that is when Christ-followers will experience corporate worship along with solid biblical teaching from God-appointed pastors and teachers. The exercise part of this equation, as it relates to the local church, is talking about active involvement and volunteering, versus a passive role of just warming a seat as a spectator.

Regarding nourishment, the pastor is there to teach and feed you the Word of God. Pastors do two things, *feed* and *lead*. As far as feeding, Scripture (God's Word) is your spiritual nourishment.

1 Peter 2:2

> Like newborn infants, long for the pure spiritual milk (of the word - NASB), that by it you may grow up into salvation.

1 Timothy 4:6

> Nourished on the truths of the faith and of the good teaching that you have followed. (NIV)

Matthew 4:4

> Man shall not live by bread alone, but by every word that comes from the mouth of God.

When you attend church, you are hearing the Word being preached to you, and that Word is spiritual nourishment that will help you to grow.

Nourishment, however, is not the only thing that you need to produce growth. As we've seen, the other component is exercise. What happens in the natural if you have constant intake of food, but no exercise? You get fat! The equation would be like this:

Nourishment + Inactivity = Fat

This too is true for the spiritual as well as the natural. Knowledge intake without application or exercise produces spiritual fatness. Maybe that is why the New International Version renders 1 Corinthians 8:1, *knowledge puffs up*!

In the natural, we love overweight people, but they wouldn't be our first choice going on a mission or taking a hill in warfare. The same is true in spiritual terms. We love and appreciate spiritually overweight people, people who have a lot of knowledge but aren't involved; but when it comes to the successful operation of the local church, they can't be counted on. Why? Because they never exercise their knowledge of God and His kingdom, it's all in their head and never transferred to their hands and feet. It seems they know everything about intercessory prayer but in the final analysis, never attend the prayer meeting (I mean the real kind of prayer meeting, the kind where they actually pray). Helping the church stay clean and tidy, greeting someone at the door, handing out a church bulletin, passing an offering basket, or holding a baby in the nursery is below their dignity…just not spiritual enough. They have more important matters to attend to—reading Bible commentaries and parsing Greek verbs!

Just because someone has a lot of biblical knowledge doesn't mean they are spiritually mature. The Corinthians are a good example of this. Here's how the Apostle Paul described them.

This group had a lot of knowledge.

1 Corinthians 1:5

> In every way you were enriched in him in all speech and **all knowledge**.

Additionally, the Corinthians weren't lacking in gifts and talent either.

1 Corinthians 1:7

> You are not lacking in any gift.

So here's a group of Christians that are full of knowledge and gifts. But how did the Apostle Paul describe these Corinthians just two chapters later?

1 Corinthians 3:1-2

> But I, brothers, could not address you as spiritual people, but as people of the flesh, as **infants in Christ**. I fed you with milk, not solid food, for you were not ready for it. And even now you are not yet ready.

Paul called them babies and that they weren't spiritual. They had a lot of knowledge and gifts, but they weren't experiencing spiritual maturity!

If you are not exercising, you are not going to grow. If you are not going to grow, you are not going to flourish. Someone might say, "I thought you said that growth depends on being planted in the house of the Lord." I did, but growth is dependent on all three things: being planted in the house of the Lord, nourishment, and exercise. What is the relationship between these three? The nourishment and exercise are supposed to be happening when planted in the house of the Lord, the local church!

1 Thessalonians 2:11-12

> For you know how, like a father (pastor) with his children (congregation), we exhorted each one of you and encouraged you and charged you (preaching, nourishment) to walk (exercise) in a manner worthy of God, who calls you into his own kingdom and glory.

That is what is supposed to be happening in a local church. Growth doesn't occur by just hearing the Word of God. Growth occurs by hearing and DOING the Word of God. When you both hear and do, you'll flourish.

James 1:25

> But the one who looks into the perfect law, the law of liberty (nourishment), and perseveres, being no hearer who forgets but a doer who acts (exerciser), he **will be blessed** (flourish) **in his doing** (exercising).

Notice the last phrase of this verse: **shall be blessed in his doing.** "Blessed" means that you will flourish and bear fruit. "In his doing" speaks of exercise.

You see, you are not blessed in the HEARING of the Word of God, you are only blessed in the DOING of the Word of God. I used to tell my congregation, "Don't ever tell me that my sermon 'blessed you.' That sermon didn't bless you until you do it!"

Philippians 4:9

> What you have learned and received and heard and seen in me—**practice these things**, and the God of peace will be with you.

If you are not exercising your knowledge, you will not grow, flourish or yield fruit. It's just that simple.

Did you know that it's possible that knowledge, which is a good thing, can turn out to be unfruitful (doesn't produce fruit).

2 Peter 1:8

> For if these qualities are yours and are increasing, they keep you from **being ineffective or unfruitful in the knowledge** of our Lord Jesus Christ.

It's possible for knowledge to be unfruitful! The New International Version has, "ineffective and unproductive in your knowledge." The New American Standard Bible is more direct, using the word "useless," —you won't be "useless nor unfruitful in the true knowledge of our Lord Jesus Christ." Knowledge is ineffective, unfruitful, and downright useless, if it's not acted or exercised upon.

Churches are full of people sitting there doing nothing and wondering why they're not thriving. It's no mystery to me why they're not. They have violated biblical principles of growth and fruit-bearing.

Remember—flourishing depends on growth, and to have growth you must be planted, along with having both components of nutrition and exercise. Without the exercise, you will not bear fruit, thrive or flourish.

Chapter 4

Choosing or Leaving a Church

We have talked about being planted in the house of the Lord and getting both nourishment and exercise there. These are important principles to understand in order to flourish. The word *planted* speaks of putting down roots and permanency. Years ago, family members would live their whole lives committed to one local church. Things have changed drastically since then. Now it's common for people to change churches every two or three years or more often! This is the opposite of being planted.

Because church-hopping is such a major problem, I want to spend some time dealing with some issues pertaining to choosing or leaving a local church. This information will help you in your relationship to the church and will serve as a foundation for the material that follows.

Choosing a Church

The Word of God is not silent about principles dealing with choosing or leaving a local church. Sometimes we have glossed over these verses and their much needed nuggets of truth. A chapter that deals with the Body of Christ and how its members interrelate with one another is 1 Corinthians 12. This is a beautiful chapter that compares the Body of Christ, the church, to a human body. Just as a human body is made up various parts with different functions, so is the church.

1 Corinthians 12:12, 18

> For just as the body is one and has many members, and all the members of the body, though many, are one body, so it is with Christ. ... But as it is, God arranged the members in the body, **each one** of them, **as he chose.**

Notice that it's God who places believers into local churches just as He desires, not as we desire. In other words, the choice of where you go to church and what you do there belongs to God, not you. He places people where He wants them to be. You're not supposed to decide all by yourself which church you'll attend. You are to seek the direction of God through the Holy Spirit on the matter. When you receive that direction from God, then you are to obey that leading, connect to that church, and get "planted."

When I was growing up, I remember a five-second TV public service announcement in the 1960s that said, "Go to the church of your choice." The motive behind that PSA was right, but scripturally speaking, it was wrong. We're not supposed to go to the church of our choice, we're supposed to go to the church of God's choice!

1 Corinthians 12:24

> **God** has so composed the body, giving greater honor to the part that lacked it.

God "composes" the body as He desires. The word "composed" here is the same Greek word that is translated "mixed" in Hebrews 4:2 in the King James Version, where it says, *but the word preached did not profit them, not being mixed with faith in them that heard it.* It's God who composes, mixes and mingles believers into His Body, the church, just as HE desires, as HE wills, not as we will. Why does God place, compose and mix the members of His body where He wants? One verse later...

1 Corinthians 12:25

> **That there may be no division in the body**, but that the members may have the same care for one another.

Evidently, there are some people who would best fit in some churches that, if they were in some other church, it would cause division. God knows where you will best fit. When I was pastoring (I'm not pastoring now), I had to remind myself occasionally that, as good as I thought the church I pastored was, everyone in the city was not called by God to join it. I didn't like admitting that, but it was true. God knows the best local church for you to join. Your job is to seek Him diligently concerning which local church He would have you be a part of.

One of the principles for being led by God and getting results in prayer is found in 2 Corinthians 5:7, where we're told to *walk by faith, not by sight.* We normally apply this to answered prayer, divine healing and other situations, but we never seem to apply it to choosing or leaving a local church. The majority of Christians are moved and led by their feelings and preferences, rather than God's direction through sensing the leading of His Spirit. Whenever you are led by emotions, feelings and personal preferences, you will miss God every time! I don't care how it looks in the natural, the natural will fool you. You should not be choosing or leaving a church based on natural circumstances, feelings or personal preferences.

If you're attending a church because it's closest to you, you're wrong. If you're attending a church because it has the best facilities, you're wrong. If you're attending a church because it has the best-looking singles group, you're wrong. If you're attending a church because it has the best worship band along with stage lighting, you're wrong. If you're attending a church because it has the kind of activities you prefer, you're wrong. If you're attending a church because it has the best speakers and musical artists, you're wrong. All of those things are based on the typical American consumerism mentality that, unfortunately, has seeped into Christian culture. In short, if you're led by the natural, you will miss God as far as day and night. The bottom line is: Where does God want you?

The same principles of walking by faith and not by sight apply to choosing or leaving a church as well as prayer, healing or anything else. Leaving a church to join another should be for only one reason...because you were legitimately and genuinely directed by God to do so. You have no spiritual right to leave a church because you didn't get your own way or were offended about something. If you go by the natural, you will miss God every time.

I find four biblical exceptions to that principle:

1. If obvious heresy is being preached.
2. If you simply can't agree with the pastor's vision.
3. If the God's Word is not truly being preached there.
4. If the presence of God is not there (church is going on, but God isn't there—they have the form of spirituality but deny it's power and presence—2 Timothy 3:5).

I find no scriptural basis for remaining in a church where the Word of God is not truly being preached or where God's presence isn't there and it's spiritually dead and dry. There is a principle that I see in Psalm 23 that touches on this.

Psalm 23:1- 2

The Lord is my shepherd; I shall not want (lack). He makes me lie down in **green pastures**. He leads me (His presence) beside **still waters.**

The Good Shepherd always leads His sheep to green pastures and still waters. "Green pastures" and "still waters" speak of lush vegetation where the sheep will be adequately fed and nourished. The Lord, the Shepherd, does not lead His sheep into dry, dead, or barren pastures! John 10:10 says that Jesus came to give us life, and that more abundantly. He also said in John 6:63 that His words are spirit and they are life. So find a church that feeds you and has life.

We're to attend a local church, not based on our own preferences, but on being sensitive to the Holy Spirit's leading—*God arranged the members in the body, each one of them,* ***as he chose*** (1 Corinthians 12:18).

William Chadwick, in his book *Stealing Sheep - The Church's Hidden Problems with Transfer Growth* (InterVarsity Press, 2001, pg 40), talks about this:

> Paul goes onto argue that legally we have become the property of God. We have been bought with a price; thus we are not our own (1 Cor 6:20) but the property of him who saved us. Our freedom is totally subject to God's sovereignty. It is not unreasonable to assume, then, that Christ, the head of the church, might have a plan and a mission for each person he has purchased to be in his kingdom. I am implying that the body has been <u>carefully</u> arranged. Divine appointment, if you will, goes into the development of each church, each part of the body.

If we have been bought with a price, and we're not our own, and 1 Corinthians 12 clearly says that God is the one who mixes and composes the body as HE desires, then our task is to seek Him as to where He would have us to be.

This principle of God choosing where you should worship is not new to the New Testament.

Deuteronomy 12:5-6

> But you shall seek **the place that the Lord your God will choose** out of all your tribes to put his name and make his habitation there. There you shall go, and there you shall bring your burnt offerings and your sacrifices, your tithes

Deuteronomy 26:1-2

> When you come into the land that the Lord your God is giving you...you shall take some of the first of all the fruit of the ground (the tithe), which you harvest from your land that the Lord your God is giving you, and you shall put it in a basket, and you shall **go to the place that the Lord your God will choose**, to make his name to dwell there.

No, don't go to the church of your choice, go to the church of God's choice.

Leaving a Church

You need to be very certain that it's God's guidance that you are following when choosing or leaving a local church. And...you need to be very careful that you are telling the truth about your reasons for leaving a church if you feel as though you need to do that.

Many times, people will play the “God card” for leaving a church, the “God told me so.” They will say something like, "Well, we just sense God leading us to a new church." That’s great if it were true, but later I hear through the grapevine that they really left because they got offended or didn’t agree with something. So if you say that God led you to a new church, make sure you are speaking the truth. "Tom, are you implying that Christians would lie?" I’m not implying that at all, I’m flat-out telling you that.

Ephesians 4:25

> Therefore, having put away falsehood, let each one of you speak the truth with his neighbor, for we are members one of another.

Paul was not talking here to unbelievers, He was talking to Christians! The New Living Translation puts Ephesians 4:25 this way:

> So stop telling lies. Let us tell our neighbors the truth, for we are all parts of the same body.

Christians speak with falsehood quite a bit, so make sure you are being honest with yourself and others if you say, "God led me to leave and go to a different church."

When God moves or leads, things are done ethically, cleanly, above board, and with unity and integrity. If leaving a church isn’t done this way, it wasn't done in a godly way. When it comes to sheep changing sheepfolds, do you think God is going to do it in such a way that it's hidden, shady, underhanded, dirty or results in strife or division? No! He said in 1 Corinthians 12:24-25 that, when He mixes or mingles people into different parts of the body (churches), it will produce a caring for one another, not division.

In Ephesians 4:11 (God gave pastors to the church), the word for "pastors" is the Greek word *poimen*, which is translated every other time as "shepherd." Plainly speaking, the pastor is God's under-shepherd over the flock. 1 Peter 5:4 speaks of Jesus being the "Chief Shepherd". Both Acts 20:28 and 1 Peter 5:2 speak of people within a congregation as being "the flock." These are biblical terms and for a good reason—they perfectly describe the place and function of a pastor and congregation. God has placed "under-shepherds" (the pastors) over the "flock" (the congregation), and these pastors are a physical representation of the unseen Chief Shepherd. Now, if the Chief Shepherd is going to move one of His sheep from one sheepfold to another, do you think He would keep that information from His under-shepherds? Of course not!

Hebrews 13:17

> Obey your leaders and submit to them, **for they are keeping watch over your souls, as those who will have to give an account**. Let them do this with joy and not with groaning, for that would be of no advantage to you.

In speaking of what pastor-shepherds do, notice the words "for they are keeping watch over your souls, as those who will have to give an account." Your pastor is commissioned by God to watch over you and will someday have to give an account directly to God for how he or she pastored and took care of you. If that pastor is accountable for you, why would the Chief Shepherd keep him or her in the dark about a very significant change with you leaving that sheepfold or congregation? Scripturally, that pastor has the right to know if you are either attaching yourself to their church or if you are leaving their church. By far, this is not the case with most people who leave a church. They just quietly slip out the back door and never show up again. No communication whatsoever. I don't believe God does things like that. And, when most people start attending a new church, it's incognito. I don't see this attitude as healthy or biblical either.

Please don't interpret this as saying that you have to ask *permission* to leave or attend a church. I am not saying that at all. What I am saying is that the pastor or his appropriate delegated leadership should be informed about what is going on with you because you are a sheep under his or her care, and he or she is accountable for you. The pastor of your church is not omniscient (all knowing). If you sense God is moving you to another local church, you should go to the pastor or someone else in official leadership in the church and tell them about it. It doesn't have to be an appointment necessarily. It doesn't have to be long and dragged out. It is a simple courtesy of communication with the leader. When God does things, He does them ethically, cleanly, above board, with purity and integrity. All of this floating around from one church to another isn't from God.

Most people leave a church because they don't agree with something or have been offended about something. Question: What is the will of God when it comes to being offended?

Matthew 18:15-17

> If your brother sins against you (or your church offends you in some way), go and tell him his fault, between you and him alone. If he listens to you, you have gained your brother. But if he does not listen, take one or two others along with you, that every charge may be established by the evidence of two or three witnesses. If he refuses to listen to them, tell it to the church. And if he refuses to listen even to the church, let him be to you as a Gentile and a tax collector.

I think Matthew 18:15-17 is the most ignored passage in the Bible. That's probably an exaggeration, but maybe not by much. Here it says "go and tell him." This means go to them personally. This is important because these days, if this step is taken (and it generally isn't), it's done by email. Usually Christians are too afraid (I'm tempted to use the word *chicken*, but I won't) to do it the Bible way, face-to-face. I cannot count all the little notes and emails I've received that say something like this: "Pastor Tom, I won't be coming to your church anymore, but I surely do love you! I just believe God is leading me out." That kind of email leaves me with lots of questions. When I see the person, I'll say, "Was something wrong? What was the matter?" By far, almost 100% of the time, they will say something like, "Oh, no, everything's fine, we just felt the Holy Spirit leading us to a new church." Later you find out that they were mad or in disagreement about something.

Folks, let's put away falsehood and speak truth.

Ephesians 4:15

> Rather, **speaking the truth in love**, we are to **grow up** in every way into him who is the head, into Christ,

We're to speak the truth in love. And isn't it interesting that it connects speaking the truth in love with spiritual growth? Part of maturity is being able to go personally to someone and have that uncomfortable chat. It's awkward, it's not fun, it may even be a little painful, but it's a sign of being mature. If you're having a problem with this kind of thing, it would behoove you to read Henry Cloud and John Townsend's book, *How to Have That Difficult Conversation—Gaining the Skills for Honest and Meaningful Conversation* (2015, Zondervan).

That is the Bible way of doing things. Paul said to do this because we're members of one another (Ephesians 4:25). Why did Paul say, *because we are members of one another*? Because when God placed us in the same body, the same local church, we are family and have a commitment to be truthful with each other, we're to care for one another (1 Corinthians 12:25). It's a matter of having integrity, honesty, and truthfulness. And I repeat, God has commissioned your pastor to watch over your soul as one who will give an account.

God wants your pastor or leader to know what's going on with you. There's a verse from Proverbs that I believe directly applies to pastors and church leaders.

Proverbs 27:23

> Know well the condition of your flocks, and give attention to your herds.

Your pastor is accountable to watch over you, to know your condition well, and pay attention to you. If he or she has that kind of responsibility, don't you think God would want them to be informed as to whether you are part of his flock or not? The principle is this: Inform your pastor (or delegated leadership) as to whether you are leaving or now attending his or her church.

Remember, don't choose a church by your feelings based on the natural or your personal preferences. And don't leave a church going by your feelings based on the natural. Attend and/or leave a church because God told you to do it, and don't let that be just an excuse, playing the "God card." Remember also, that in joining or leaving a church, you are accountable to personally inform your pastor or other delegated church leadership as to what God is doing in your life because, after all, the leadership is accountable for you.

I want to conclude this chapter by letting you in on something: ***There is no such thing as a perfect church!***

"Well, I was in a church once and got hurt!" Listen, everybody has had problems somewhere at some time or another. Does that mean God has waived His plan for sheep being in sheepfolds under shepherds and is now allowing you to play "Lone Ranger?" No! God hasn't given you a pass to attend *Bedside Assembly* or

Springs of Life just because you had a bad experience somewhere. It's not God's will for you to attend *Saint Mattress* with *Pastor Pillow* and *Brother Sheets* just because you got bothered about something. I don't care what church you attend, it's not perfect. If you are looking for a perfect local church, forget it, you'll never find it. The early church had a lot of problems too (1 Cor. 3:1-3, 11:18), but Paul's advice was never for a bunch of them to leave and start another church down the road. His advice was for them to stick in there and to grow up.

The truth is, you are either part of the problem or part of the solution. Which is it? Your actions will locate you. If you murmur, complain, gossip, and spread negative seeds of discontent, you are part of the problem. But if you refuse to talk about it and simply commit yourself to prayer, you are part of the answer. God never designed your ears to double as garbage cans. If someone wants to talk about problems they have with the church, you need to say, "Hey, let's not talk about this, let's pray together right now for the pastor and church, that God would bless them and give them wisdom." That will shut up the gossip 99 percent of the time and sometimes will bring about a change of heart in the gossiper. Also, if you listen to the gossip without speaking up against it, you become just as guilty as the one spreading it. Proverbs 6 talks about seven things the Lord hates. Here's the last one mentioned.

Proverbs 6:19

One who **sows** discord among brothers.

Notice that it uses the word *sows.* That's a good word to use because words are seeds that can take root in someone's heart. There are people in our churches who specialize in sowing negative seeds of strife and discontent, and you need to make a decision as to whether you are going to let them sow these seeds into you or not. Seeds of discontent, whether you speak them or just hear them, will still take root in your heart. Don't allow yourself to get into a position of hearing "garbage." Shut it down immediately.

Every church you have ever attended or ever will attend has some problems. Are you going to help solve the problems, or are you going to just get upset and storm out to another church? God wants us to grow up and be part of the solution, to be agents of healing and restoration. We are to be "planted in the house of the Lord," not jerked out of the ground and moved somewhere else every two or three years.

CHAPTER 5

Fitted in the Body

God wants you to thrive, succeed and flourish spiritually (and for that matter, in all realms of life). Flourishing is contingent upon growth. Growth depends on being planted somewhere and two additional things—nutrition and exercise. Growth and exercise will take place when you are "planted in the house of the Lord." Being planted in the local church is the opposite of not going to church anywhere or floating from church to church. "Planted" speaks of putting down roots...a degree of permanency.

The above paragraph is a summary of the first four chapters, which were designed as an introduction to what is contained in these next four. I have endeavored to build a foundation that will serve to promote greater understanding for the rest of this book. Unless you get a firm grasp on what has been said thus far, the remainder of the book may not make much sense to you.

There are no substitutes for the local church. Online sermons or podcasts are no substitute for regular attendance at a good local church. Watching Sunday morning TV pastors is not a substitute for the local church. Parachurch bible studies are not a substitute. Watching a YouTube or online church service is not a substitute. Your small group is not a substitute. Even personal prayer and Bible study is not a substitute for the local church. There are no substitutes for the local church. All those things are fine, but they are not a substitute for the local church. When we look directly at the New Testament, we see the universal church (the church around the world) broken down into individual local churches, so on a "where the rubber meets the road" practicality, the local church is our real focus.

There was a time when people began to wonder if the local church would be superseded by parachurch organizations (Christian ministries not associated with a particular local church). But that is complete foolishness. God ordained the local church, and He has never rescinded or replaced it. I believe parachurch ministries and organizations are great. I thank God for them. God raised them up for unique purposes that local churches were not involved with on a big scale. When churches weren't ministering to the poor as they should, God raised up the Salvation Army. When churches weren't reaching high school kids, God raised up Young Life and Youth for Christ. When churches weren't reaching college students, God raised up InterVarsity and Campus Crusade for Christ. There's no doubt that God's hand is on these and many other parachurch ministries, too many to mention here. But…they are not substitutes for the local church, and they will tell you that.

Someone most likely will think, "Aw, he's just saying these things because he wants big churches." Of course I want big churches. I want all size churches; small, medium and large. God is all in favor of big churches. In fact, He is so in favor of it that on the Day of Pentecost, 3,000 people were born again and became part of the church at Jerusalem—all in one day (Acts 2:41). That's not bad growth. And their numbers after that increased, not week-by-week, but day-by-day (Acts 2:47). Sure I want big churches, along with small and medium size churches, but that is not why I am saying these things. I'm telling you these things so that you will flourish, prosper and succeed spiritually. You cannot flourish or bear fruit until you are planted and begin to grow. **Planted-Grow-Bear Fruit.** That's the sequence. That is just common sense, as we found out from Psalm 1 and 92. Yielding fruit comes after you are firmly planted in the Word of God and in a local church—one of God's choosing. A seed that is dug up and moved around will never produce or bear fruit. Most people who go from church to church are still spiritual babies. They would not think of themselves as babies, but that's what they really are.

Someone may say, "Well, I don't belong to a local church. My contribution or ministry is to the universal church, the Body of Christ as a whole." You may be an evangelist, or in a "field" ministry, but God still wants you joined to or working out of a good local church. Paul operated out of the church at Antioch, and I believe the same principle applies to field or mobile ministries today. Obviously, someone who is on the road all the time cannot be involved in the local church like people who have local jobs or ministries. But, when off the road, that evangelist or teacher should be at a church on Sundays, doing whatever he or she can do to contribute. The same principles that apply for the universal church apply for the local church. If God wants you to be a member of the universal church, then He also wants you to be an integral part of the local church.

God is really moving in the church, both the universal church and the local church. In both cases, God wants a strong body of believers. Most churches that I've seen are full of people who just sit around and watch the precious few do all the work. Growth in the church is fine but, if attendance goes from 100 to 1,000 people and the extra 900 don't do anything, what good is that added attendance? Babies who stay babies should not be viewed as church growth. God doesn't want spectators, He wants players.

I am believing for a time when our churches will have absolutely no pew-sitters. In the church which I pioneered and pastored, I tried to promote people who were already busy and engaged somehow. You will find this to be a principle all through the bible. God chose Moses and David while they were working as shepherds. Elijah chose Elisha while he was in the field working (1 Kings 19:19,20). Jesus chose His disciples while they were working; Peter and Andrew while they were fishing, James and John while they were mending their fishing nets (Matt. 4:18-22), and Matthew while he was sitting at a table collecting taxes (Matthew 9:9). We have a lot of benchwarmers in our churches, but Hebrews 12:1 says that we're all in the race. You can't begin to run until you enlist in the race. Enlisting to help in your pastor's vision is a form of getting into that spiritual race and helping the church run for the goal. Habakkuk 2:2 says that we're to *run with the vision*! God doesn't want bystanders reciting the vision, He wants runners running with the vision.

God wants you under a shepherd and in a sheepfold of sheep. If you are not attached to a local fold (congregation), you are in a position of being vulnerable to the attack of wolves. An isolated sheep is easy prey to a predator. As a pastor, I have seen people time and again who stopped going to church and began to drift away from their walk with God. It never turned out well.

I heard the story of a Jewish man in Poland a century ago, who stopped attending his synagogue. One winter night, his rabbi came to visit. He came into the house, sat down by the fire with the man, but didn't say a word. After a long time of both staring at the fireplace, the rabbi took the tongs, picked out one red-hot glowing coal from the fire, and set it out all by itself on the hearth. They both just stared as the ember grew cold and went out. Then the rabbi got up and left, not saying a word. The next Saturday the rabbi saw the man sitting in the congregation—he had gotten the message.

The Christian version is somewhat similar, but with a little twist. A pastor went to visit a house of a church attender whom he hadn't seen in quite a while. He knocked on the door, but no one came, even though the house lights were on. He took out a piece of paper and wrote out the words from Revelation 3:20— "Behold I stand at the door and knock, if anyone hears me, and opens the door, I'll come in and have fellowship with them," and stuck the note in the door. The next Sunday in the offering, he saw a communication card from the lady that lived at the house, and she simply wrote, “Genesis 3:10—I heard your voice and I was afraid because I was naked; and I hid myself.”

Fitted Into the Body

Again, let me say that God wants you to flourish, but you only flourish when you grow. How do you grow spiritually? Most people give the standard answer.

1 Peter 2:2

> Like newborn babies, long for the pure milk of the word, so that by it you may grow in respect to salvation. (NASB)

This, of course, is true, but it’s not the whole truth. Don't take *a* truth and make it *the* truth. As we’ve seen, taking in nourishment is not the only component of growth. Some people think the only way to grow is to read the bible all the time. If that were true, every seminary student would be a spiritual giant, and that is definitely not true. It’s nutrition plus exercise that produces growth.

Let’s look at a very important passage from Ephesians 4:11-16. The passage touches on the idea of growth in every verse, but we’ll break it up to make some important points.

Ephesians 4:11-12

> And he gave the apostles, the prophets, the evangelists, the shepherds (NIV, NASB & NLT:

> "pastors") and teachers, to equip the saints for the work of ministry, **for building up the body of Christ.**

God gave pastor-shepherd-teachers to the church "for the building up the body of Christ." That speaks of growth. I think it would be obvious that a Christian would have to sit under the teaching and leading of a pastor in order for that to happen to the fullest degree.

Ephesians 4:13

> until we all attain to the unity of the faith and of the knowledge of the Son of God, **to mature manhood,** to the measure of the stature of the fullness of Christ,

Clearly, this is talking about growing with the goal of spiritual maturity.

Ephesians 4:14

> so that we may **no longer be children**, tossed to and fro by the waves and carried about by every wind of doctrine, by human cunning, by craftiness in deceitful schemes.

The result is that we *no longer be children.* That also indicates growth. Children and young-in-the-faith Christians are easily suckered into false teaching and ideas. But as one matures, they're able to decipher true from false doctrine. Keep in mind, however, that this is in the context of spiritual growth that comes from sitting under the ministry of the apostle, prophet, evangelist, pastor and teacher.

Ephesians 4:15

> Rather, speaking the truth in love, **we are to grow up** in every way into him who is the head, into Christ,

Helping believers to "grow up in every way" is why God wants believers to be under the care of pastors. Acts 2:42 says that the believers "devoted themselves to the apostles' teaching." This happened when believers assembled together, and was before there were any pastors or local churches...there were just the Apostles. Pastors came later, but the principle remains—they devoted themselves to regularly being fed the Word of God with other believes in the local assembly. A careful reading of Acts 2:42-47 will show that the believers did this continually.

Ephesians 4:16

> from whom the whole body, **joined and held together** by every joint with which it is equipped, when each part is working properly, **makes the body grow** so that it builds itself up in love.

As the body comes together, is fed the Word of God through God-called men and women in ministry, and as they do their part (we'll cover this in the next chapter), growth is the result, both individually and corporately.

Let's look at those words, "**joined and held together**." The King James Version says, "**fitly joined together**." In the Greek language (the New Testament was written in Greek), it literally means "**to join closely together**" (Strong's Greek definition #4883), also "**fitly framed together**." Vincent Word Studies says these words "**being fitted**" literally mean "**fitly joined or compacted**." Vincent Word Studies goes on to say that in the Greek, the present participle denotes "present, continuous progress." In other words, "joined closely together" never stops, it's to go on as long as we live.

God's will for all believers is that they be joined or closely compacted together in the body (church). Does that describe you and your relationship to your local church? The way to growth, and then to flourishing, is first of all, to be fitted closely together in a church. Those verses don't say *loosely joined*, they say *closely joined*. How do you know the difference? I'll give you a clue...you are not closely joined together if you only show up at church every two, three or four weeks! And to poo-poo or negate this important principle that we see in Ephesians 4 adversely affects your spiritual growth which, in turn, adversely affects your flourishing.

This same Greek word (fitted or fit together) is also found in Ephesians 2:21.

Ephesians 2:21

(Christ Jesus), in whom **the whole structure**, being **joined together**, **grows** into a holy temple in the Lord.

The *holy temple of the Lord* here is not you individually, but the entire body, the church. Notice that in this verse growth is connected with being fitted together with one another. The local church is a spiritual building which will flourish only when believers are fitted closely together with one another. It says *the whole structure* is to be this way. In other words, not one stone or board in this building is exempt. All stones or boards in the temple are to be joined together, and from our definition mentioned earlier...closely together. This is God's way, His design.

1 Peter 2:5

> You yourselves like living stones are being built up as a spiritual house.

Each one of you is to be a stone in God's spiritual house called "the church." This is true not just for the universal church, but the local church as well. What's good for the universal church is good for the local church. The same principles apply.

Fish swim in schools, birds and sheep gather in flocks. I'm a certified scuba diver and love to see schools of fish moving together. Did you ever see an entire school of fish swim together? They are so in unison that when they change direction, it looks like a whole wall changing direction, not just a lot of individual fish. Have you ever seen videos of a "murmuration" of starlings in the UK? Just go to YouTube sometime and search for "murmuration of starlings." It will boggle your mind. The Body of Christ should be the same way.

We're not supposed to be "lone rangers" staying isolated and doing our own thing. We're not supposed to be "cruisa-matics," cruising over to this church, then cruising over to that church. That is what is meant in 1 Corinthians 12:18 when it says, *But now God has placed (fitted) the members, each one of them, in the body (church), just as He desired.*

Why is it that 90% of Americans believe in God and only 10% go to church regularly (I don't believe the statistics that say 30-40% go to church)? I think it's for one of four possible reasons.

Why people don't go to church:

1. They are ignorant of the very principles taught in this book. Therefore they see spiritual growth as an individual thing not connected to community.

2. They don't take the Lordship of Jesus Christ seriously. In other words, they know it's God's will but are just being disobedient.

3. They don't feel like they're getting any value from church attendance. Of course, if the church is dead, dry or the Word of God is not being fully preached there, that could be the reason. If that's the case, find a church that preaches God's Word and where God's presence is actually sensed.

4. They have suckered into being conformed to American culture by not valuing Sunday (or Saturday, whatever you're into) as a Sabbath, a day set aside for both rest and corporate worship. Consequently, they allow recreation and other activities to take precedent over church attendance.

I noticed an incremental morphing of society through the 1980s, 1990s and on into the present, that more and more recreational activities are being scheduled on Sunday mornings. This was no accident, it was and is part of a well-developed strategy of the devil (along with atheists, humanists and secularists). It was incremental, but the awareness to me came suddenly—"Hey, all the kids baseball, soccer and football games are scheduled for Sundays mornings!" Sunday mornings became the time to do whatever you "felt" like doing.

As a pastor, I remember talking to people who told me they didn't attend regularly because, "Well...Sunday mornings is our time for sleeping in, going out to breakfast, walking the dog, going grocery shopping, taking a jog, reading the Sunday morning paper, or taking little Buford to little league."

Let me explain how this works. When you miss church to take little Buford to little league or little-guy soccer (or whatever) on Sunday mornings, you have just both taught and modeled to Buford that recreation comes before God, that church is not as important as these other recreational activities. Twelve years later when Buford doesn't give a rip about God or the things of God, parents scratch their heads and wonder why. And when they come and ask me about it, I feel like saying (but never do), "Hey, take Buford to his little league coach and get counsel from him!"

Friends, Jesus died for the church so that we could get connected to God and one another! And it's His will we get and stay connected, closely connected, to a good church.

Hebrews 10:25

> **Some people have gotten out of the habit of meeting for worship, but we must not do that.** We should keep on encouraging each other, especially since you know that the day of the Lord's coming is getting closer.

To me, "disconnected Christian" is an oxymoron because in the New Testament, it's unheard of. An oxymoron is a term with two words that contradict each other, like: *jumbo shrimp*, *loose tights*, *tight slacks*, *pretty ugly*, *sanitary landfill*, *act naturally*, *found missing*, *legally drunk*, *alone together*, *rap music*, *military intelligence*, *12-ounce pound cake*, or *airline food*. Well, "disconnected Christian" doesn't make sense from the standpoint of Scripture. It's an oxymoron.

In 1994, when pastoring in Rochester, New York, I saw an ad in the *Genesee Valley Penny Saver*, which is a little local newspaper with articles, events, classifieds and advertisements. In the issue, I found this ad:

> **CHRISTIAN COUPLE**, mid 50's (born again, but not church goers) desires fellowship w/ Christian couple. Interests: Reading, gardening, cooking, wild birds, woodwork. Possibly Bible study. Write: Sheep. P.O. Box ______, __________ NY

I still have the ad. Basically, this couple was saying, "We want the benefits of being in a church without actually being in a church."

That's the American dream—receiving the benefits of connection without actually being connected. This is American consumerism. We want perks without pay-in. We want pastors to perform the weddings of our children and funerals of our parents, but we refuse to be connected to the church in any regular or meaningful way. Americans are funny this way, they crave community without taking steps to connect to community. It's intriguing to me.

It's time we move from ***believer*** to ***belonger***. Each one of us is to be fitted closely together into a local body of believers. If you're not, it's very possible that this is the reason you're not flourishing. There is a divine order to everything, and God's order is that you *join closely together* with other believers in a church and then start to grow and flourish.

Romans 12:4-5

> For as in (fitted in) one body we have many members, and the members do not all have the same function (the second word in the title of this book), so we, though many, are one body in Christ, and individually members one of another.

We truly express that we're "members of one another" only when we, in a real and practical way, are fitted in the body. These verses are saying the same thing as the verses we read in Ephesians 4 and 1 Corinthians 12—that all the members are to be fitted into the body so they can function there, each in their proper God-designated place.

Being "fitted" into a local church speaks of the nutrition element of our growth equation. When you are regularly and consistently attending a church, you will be hearing the Word of God on a regular, consistent basis which will be your intake of spiritual food—not your only intake, but a big part of it (individually we should be reading and studying Scripture daily). We see an example of this in the early church of Acts.

Acts 2:41-42

> So those who received his word were baptized, and there were added that day about three thousand souls. And they devoted themselves to the apostles' teaching and the fellowship, to the breaking of bread and the prayers.

The first thing believers did after they got saved was join with other believers and sit under the teaching (nourishment) of the Apostles, along with constant group fellowship and prayer. This is what made the body of believers in the book of Acts so strong. What was the result of this continual teaching and fellowship?

Acts 2:46-47

> And day by day (not once a month), attending the temple together and breaking bread in their homes, they received their food with glad and generous hearts, praising God and having favor with all the

people. **And the Lord added to their number** day by day those who were being saved.

Kingdom growth was the inevitable result.

Benefits of 'Fitting'

Many don't realize it, but there are many benefits to regularly attending a local church (fitting). Here are just a few.

1. **Teaching.**
   - Teaching from God-called and equipped teachers.
   - Balanced teaching—otherwise, you study only what you want to, creating imbalance.

2. **Leading.**
   - Pastors are called by God to both feed and lead. If not connected to a local church, who leads you?

3. **Protection.**
   - Direction—Protection for your life's direction and the steps you are taking.
   - Doctrine—Protection from false doctrine.

4. **Fellowship.**
   - Becomes a place to know and be known.
   - A place to meet and create new friends.
   - A place to gather with others to have fun and enjoy life.

5. **A place of community to express and receive love, care and support.**
   - We want to express love, care and support, but many times we aren't aware of others' needs.
   - By attending a church we become aware and therefore can reach out to those in need, and they to us.

6. **A place to discover and express your gifts and passions.**
   - A place to regularly serve God with your God-given gifts.
   - A place where others can help you discover and affirm your spiritual gifts.

7. **A place to invite the lost.**
   - There must be a place where we can say to someone, "Come and see." John 1:46

8. **A place to experience the rewards of team and teamwork.**
   - David had his band of fellow warriors. Jesus had His twelve. Paul had Timothy, Silas, Barnabus, Titus and John Mark.
   - As we examine Scripture, we see the rewards of doing mission as a team and experiencing teamwork, instead of solo work.
   - The complaint, "I just don't know anybody," is easily remedied by believers attending a weekly small group and serving regularly with a team.

9. **A place to get involved in world missions.**

- Global evangelism and world missions starts in the local church.
- The Apostle Paul worked out of his home church in Antioch.
- People in churches catch a world vision through their prayers, giving, and short-term mission trips.

10. It enhances the journey.

- Traveling on our spiritual journey with others enhances the enjoyment of the trip.
- When I was in the Air Force stationed in southern Turkey, I took a trip to Athens, Greece. I was there alone. I toured the Acropolis, Parthenon, and Corinth. But instead of it being exhilarating, it was deflating, because I had no one to share it with.

11. Accountability and correction.

- Hebrews 13:17 - Leaders "keep watch over your souls."
- Sometimes they bring needed correction. Titus 2:15, 2 Timothy 4:2
- We shortchange ourselves when we don't avail ourselves to accountability and correction.

12. Encouragement to press on in discipleship, spiritual growth and transformation.

- Hebrews 10:24 - And let us consider how to stir up one another to love and good works.
- Not being in a local church blocks other people from helping you press on to maturity.
- The local church provides a place where others can encourage you to hang in there and grow, and experience transformation.

13. **Model community to the next generation.**
    - Having our families with us in church on a regular basis models the value of community to our children, which hopefully, impacts that generation with a love for God and His church.
    - Models and instills into your children compassion and values.

14. **A place to help in relational conflict.**
    - Matthew 18:15-18 teaches us that if we have conflict, we can bring it to church leaders who can help us resolve that conflict.

15. **Opens your thinking to new ideas and perspectives.**
    - Without the input and ideas of others, our views and perspectives become myopic (tunnel vision).
    - Being in a local church expands our thinking on many different areas, not the least of which is interpretation of Scripture.

16. **A place to experience corporate worship and God's presence.**
    - You can pray by yourself (and should), and you can worship by yourself (and should), but there is a special anointing experienced when we pray and worship together. Matthew 18:19, Acts 4:24-31.

17. **The place to help you minister to your community in the areas of benevolence, charity and social justice**

- Many people want to reach out to their community in these ways, but they don't know how or who to partner with.
- The local church becomes a great Christ-centered focal point for community outreach.

18. **Helps to calibrate you and your family's spiritual and moral compass.**
    - After living in a secular, and even ungodly environment during the week, attending church helps to recalibrate ourselves back to God and His values.

19. **Helps your family anchor to the past with Christian tradition.**
    - Whether it's baptism, communion or the seasons of Advent, Lent, Passion week—church attendance helps us to celebrate Christian traditions that are thousands of years old.

20. **Research has shown that regular church-goers are healthier, live longer lives, are happier, and have significantly less depression than non-church-goers.**
    - One can simply do an Internet search and easily find out the physical, emotional and relational benefits of attending church and living a godly lifestyle.

Here in this chapter, "fitted" speaks of the need for regular attendance in a local church. Hopefully by now we've seen in Scripture that this is God's will for all believers. But remember that the other half of the growth equation is *exercise*. We'll talk about the exercise element of growth in the next two chapters.

Chapter 6

The 'Why?' of Functioning

The word "fitted" speaks of attending or being connected to a good, local body of believers in the local church. It's the *nourishment* element of our growth equation because the local church is an important place where you're going to get fed the Word of God, which is spiritual food to help you grow, along with experiencing corporate worship, which also helps us grow in our intimacy with God. But there is more to growth than just attending church. Here in Chapter 6 we'll begin to cover the second element of our growth equation, "function." Specifically here we want to answer the question of "why?"—why are we to function—why are we to get involved and volunteer in the church?

The short answer is—because God told us to. That should be sufficient for those who truly understand what the Lordship of Jesus Christ really means. Even though that's true, it's still worth explaining this in more detail because it serves to support and inspire us for future steps in discipleship.

If just attending church was the thing that produced growth, then our churches would be full of spiritual giants, which is not the case. The *exercise* element of our growth equation comes in two forms: 1) being a doer of the Word and 2) functioning in the Body of Christ (getting off the bench as a spectator and becoming a player). Let's turn our attention again to Ephesians 4 as we examine God's will for believers to not only fit, but function.

Ephesians 4:16

> (Christ) from whom the whole body, joined and held together **by every joint with which it is equipped, when each part is working properly**, makes the body grow so that it builds itself up in love.

The New King James Version reads this way:

> (Christ) from whom the whole body, joined and knit together **by what every joint supplies**, according to **the effective working by which every part does its share**, causes growth of the body for the edifying of itself in love.

Those two phrases, **every joint with which it is equipped** (NKJV: by what every joint supplies) and **when each part is working properly** (NKJV: the effective working by which every part does its share), are the subject of this chapter.

It's not enough for you to just fit into a local church (attendance). God wants you to go a step further and function in the church as well. Vincent Word Studies says the phrase ***what every joint supplies*** literally means ***joint of the supply, which signifies a joint whose office or purpose it is to supply.*** And what is the nature of the thing every joint is to supply? The answer is found in the verse...***effective working.*** Friend, this isn't just attending a church, this is functioning (doing something) in the church. Your purpose in the body is to supply something other than just to warm a chair or give money. Notice that in this verse it says, *what **every** joint supplies*. This means that not one person is excluded from this injunction. Everyone, including you and me, should be connected to and functioning in a local body of believers.

One time I purchased a gas grill from one of those big box national hardware stores. This was a mistake for someone like me because I am not mechanically inclined. In fact, I have a sticky note on my box of nails that says, "pointy side toward wall" just to remind me how those things work. The gas grill came in a big cardboard box. On the outside of the box it said, **"Assembly Required."** You see, the box contained many individual parts, but these parts weren't "assembled." This means even though the many parts were together in the same geographical place, they really weren't connected to each other in such a way so as to perform a function. The local church is like that—the parts are together but not necessarily connected and functioning. It's only by the parts connected and functioning together that God's mission for the church is achieved. Your purpose in the Body of Christ is to supply something.

What is all of this saying? It's saying that the part you are to supply is work or contribution in some form in the local church. You are to function there. I am not talking about a physical building. I am talking about the believers IN the building, whether those believers meet in a home, store front, nice church building or anywhere else. Are you regularly attending a local church? If you are, are you functioning, working or volunteering in that church in some capacity? Are you involved? It says the proper working of **each individual part**. That leaves no one out.

I've noticed sometimes that wealthy people or people who have obvious status in the community shy away from functioning or volunteering in the church. It's almost like they feel it's below them. This isn't new. Nehemiah had this problem. When Nehemiah was rebuilding the walls of Jerusalem, at the time he needed "all hands on deck," there was a certain group of people that said, "Nah, no thanks."

Nehemiah 3:5

> The next section was repaired by the men of Tekoa, **but their nobles would not put their shoulders to the work** under their supervisors.

"Their nobles" wouldn't put their shoulders to the work. The tendency of wealthy people or people of status, is to think they are above such work. It doesn't have to be this way, it shouldn't be this way, but many times it is. For me as a pastor, there's nothing more refreshing than seeing someone "noble," someone of wealth or status, at the door greeting people, handing out a church program, helping take the offering, serving coffee or a myriad of other functions. The point...*each individual part* means there are no exceptions.

Now we can more fully see God's plan to flourish, which is for believers to fit and function in a local body. It's easier just to sit back and watch than it is to get involved in the work of the church. It's easier for many people to just show up and give their tithes and offerings than it is to get involved in the church. Coming in and working the sound board, singing or playing an instrument in the band, taking care of a baby in the nursery, teaching our children about God, handing out a church program to people walking in, or emptying trash after the service involves work and something called "commitment." The only thing most people do is sit in a pew or chair and look at the back of someone else's head for an hour or so. That's not too demanding.

I believe, as seen in Scripture, that God's will is that you get involved and start to work arm-in-arm with other people in the church in whatever capacity. This is why most churches never grow. The congregation generally leaves the work up to the pastor and a few diligent members. One of the goals I had for the church I pioneered and pastored was 100% workers, that everyone who attended would step up and volunteer in some way. We never reached that goal, probably 40-50%, but it was something we were always shooting for. Ephesians 4:16 says that if everyone will fit and function in the church, it will result in the growth of the body.

In 1 Corinthians 12, the church is compared to a physical human body. Let me ask you a question: If your body is without an arm, could you function to the same degree of efficiency as you would if you had that arm? Absolutely not. You could overcome that handicap so that the same results are achieved, but more pressure will have to be placed on another part of the body that was never meant to do that work (or that much work). Handicaps can be overcome, but it means the other parts of the body work double-time. If parts have to work double-time, they may get "burned out" and stop working. I have seen this happen many times in the setting of the local church. One person will head up an area and, because he or she has no volunteers, they eventually will lose their zeal and vision and then quit. Those not doing their part will always cause more pressure on the other parts.

Here's a similar question: What is the difference between a person with no arm and a person whose arm is paralyzed and therefore not functioning? There is virtually no difference! It's the same dynamic in a church. A church without a children's church volunteer and a church with someone so gifted but who decided not to volunteer...are in the same boat. A church with no musicians and a church with musicians who don't play are in the same predicament. Each person is to work and function doing his or her part. From 1 Corinthians 12, we learn that not everyone is an eye or an ear, but everyone is something and that something is very much needed in the body, the church. You may be a greeter at the door handing out bulletins; but if that is what your part is, then do it and do it well, because you are very much needed there.

Complacency

There is a verse in Proverbs 1 that comes into play here. The way it reads in the King James Version is unfortunate.

Proverbs 1:32

The prosperity of fools shall destroy them. (KJV)

The confusion lies in the meaning of the word "prosperity." In the Hebrew (the Old Testament was written primarily in Hebrew), this word has nothing to do with our modern definition of the word prosperity (although oddly enough, there IS a connection if you think about it). It literally means "complacency." It's translated that way in numerous versions of the Bible.

The New American Standard Bible

The complacency of fools shall destroy them.

The New International Version

The complacency of fools will destroy them.

The New Living Translation

Fools are destroyed by their own complacency.

The English Standard Version

The complacency of fools destroys them.

Complacency destroys! It not only destroys churches, it destroys individuals. Complacency is one of the biggest problems in the church. Your complacency will harm you spiritually, and this is the exact opposite of our principle of *fit, function, and flourish.* Complacency means not fitting or functioning. You may flourish in your career or in other areas of your life, but not spiritually because you have ignored the will of God for your life.

You have free will, and no one, not even God Himself, can force you to fit and function in a local church, that choice is up to you. In some way, complacency destroys and degrades spiritual health. The health and growth of both the church and individual believers depends on the members of a body fitting and functioning in it. If they don't, it's not mysterious what happens: no growth or flourishing for the church or individual. Complacency destroys.

I heard a story about a college that formed an Apathy Club, even appointing officers. They created an agenda, scheduled a date on the calendar, secured the room, did a lot of advertising for their first meeting, and when that time came...no one showed up! Why? Because they were too apathetic to attend! There seems to be a spiritual sluggishness that has come into our churches. Do you remember the events related in Matthew 26:36-46 about when Jesus went to the Garden of Gethsemane before the crucifixion? He needed some prayer and moral support at that point of time, and the only thing His disciples could do was sleep. Three times Jesus found them asleep.

Matthew 26:45

Then he came to the disciples and said, "Go ahead and sleep. Have your rest. But look—the time has come. The Son of Man is betrayed into the hands of sinners. (NLT)

Jesus, in effect, was saying, "Sleep on, disciples. It's too late now." His disciples were sleeping then and, sad to say, many are sleeping now. This book, hopefully, will help awaken the sleeping disciples. It's a call to stir you up to fit and function in a local church where you are very much needed. It's time for all disciples to quit "taking their rest" and start doing what God has for them to do. You need to get this established in your mind: **You are needed.**

I have heard preachers say, "You know, folks, God doesn't need you." That is not true. Oh, in the sense of His accomplishing His great plan of redemption and end-time events, true, He is going to accomplish that whether you get involved or not. But the fact is, He does need you to get involved with establishing His kingdom here on earth. Whatever part you have to supply, it's needed and essential. There is work to be done.

In Isaiah 6:8, God had some work that needed to be done. He asked, "Whom shall I send?" Isaiah's response was "Here am I. Send me!" But many people's attitude today is, "Here am I, send someone else!" That attitude must change if we want to flourish as individuals and if the church is to grow. God is looking for people who are both willing and obedient to Him.

Isaiah 1:19

If you are **willing** and **obedient** (fit and function), you shall eat the good of the land (flourish).

Those who name Jesus Christ as their Lord and Savior should be both willing and obedient to both fit and function, and as they are, they will flourish.

Many people view the local church as the place to worship God. Of course, that is correct. That's part of it, but not all of it. Let me explain. Notice something in this next verse from Romans 1.

Romans 1:25

> They exchanged the truth about God for a lie and **worshiped and served** the creature rather than (implied: **worshipping and serving**) the Creator, who is blessed forever! Amen.

It's interesting to me that *worship* and *serving* are connected. It's not just worshipping, it's serving as well, which speaks of "service." We're to worship AND serve our Creator. The connection between worshipping and serving is very biblical. When tempted by Satan to worship him, Jesus replied:

Luke 4:8

> It is written, "You shall **worship** the Lord your God, and him only shall you **serve.**"

Again, we see the connection between worshipping and serving. When we view church as only a place to worship, but not serve, we miss the deeper level of discipleship that God would have us enter into. The reason we've been saved and set free from the bondage of sin, is to do both.

Exodus 8:1

> Then the Lord said to Moses, "Go in to Pharaoh and say to him, 'Thus says the Lord, "Let my people go, **that they may serve me.**

It's interesting that bible translations alternate between translating this Hebrew word "serve" or "worship." This means that the two ideas (*worship* and *serve*) are so connected to each other that they can be translated either way! You can't really separate them!

We've been saved to serve, not saved to sit! This means moving from worshipper only, to worshipping and serving. Now that we've been born again, God has something in mind for us to do to serve Him and expand His kingdom. The reason God blesses us is NOT just for ourselves, but to be a blessing to others.

Genesis 12:2

> And I will make of you a great nation, and **I will bless you** and make your name great, **so that you will be a blessing.**

You are blessed so that you can be a blessing to others! And God saved us not just so we could just go to heaven one day, but that we could get busy accomplishing His plan for our lives in the here and now.

Ephesians 2:10

> For we are God's masterpiece. He has created us anew in Christ Jesus, **so we can do the good things he planned for us long ago.** (NLT)

The New King James Version reads, "created in Christ Jesus for good works." Saved to serve! We're not saved BY good works, we've been saved FOR good works. And the good works we're supposed to be doing is...being joined together and working properly with all other parts in the body (Ephesians 4:16). God wants to turn spectators into players.

The Ministry of Helps

Not everyone will be on the platform teaching, singing or playing a musical instrument. Not everyone is skilled enough to run the sound or lighting board. But EVERYONE can do something, EVERYONE can help in some way.

1 Corinthians 12:28

> And God has appointed **in the church** first apostles, second prophets, third teachers, then miracles, then gifts of healing, **helping**, administrating, and various kinds of tongues.

Notice two things here; **in the church** and **helping**. God has set <u>in the church</u> a ministry called "helping!' We call it *the ministry of helps.*

It has only been in recent years that the value and meaning of "the ministry of helps" has come to prominence. Churches are coming alive as they have developed and released volunteers in the ministry of helps.

Helps in the Greek literally means **"one of the administrations in the local church by way of rendering assistance."** The pastor can't do it all. When I first started pastoring, I did everything. I was the first one there to unlock the doors, I turned up the heat, set up the chairs, lead the praise and worship service (oh dear, not good)—I mean the whole thing! It didn't take very long for me to figure out that was not going to work. A pastor cannot operate successfully without the ministry of helps in operation in his or her church. The church will not grow to any significant degree without it.

I believe insight into the relationship of the leadership of the church and the ministry of helps can be gained by observing how Jesus operated. There were many times when Jesus delegated natural tasks to His disciples. For example, in Matthew 8:23-26, Jesus and His disciples were crossing the Sea of Galilee in a boat. Jesus was asleep in the back of the boat, and the disciples were doing all the rowing. That's the ministry of helps in operation. In Matthew 14:15-20, it was the disciples who distributed the fish and the loaves of bread to the multitudes. Think about how much work was involved in distributing food to more than 5,000 people. They were operating in the ministry of helps rendering assistance.

In Matthew 21:1-3, Jesus chose two disciples to go and get a colt. This is when Jesus made His triumphal entry into Jerusalem. The two disciples were operating in the ministry of helps. In Mark 14:13-16, again Jesus sent two disciples to prepare for the Passover and secure a room and supplies. This was the ministry of helps in operation. In Acts 6:1-7, we see that the apostles learned quickly that they couldn't do everything. They delegated the waiting on tables to seven good men, and the church grew as a result.

Why should we function? Because it's God's will. Additionally, we should also function because it causes growth both in the individual and the church.

Chapter 7

The 'What?'-'Where?'-'How' of Functioning

Having touched on the 'why' of functioning, let's now turn our attention to the 'what', 'where' and 'how' of functioning.

Romans 12:4:

> For just as we have many members in (fitted in) one body, all the members do not have the same **function**.

We don't all have the same function, but we all have a function. You have a function, and you are to function in your function!

Romans 12:4-5 in the Amplified Bible says:

> For just as in one [physical] body we have many parts, and these parts do not all have the same function or special use, so we, who are many, are [nevertheless just] one body in Christ, and

individually [we are] parts one of another [mutually dependent on each other].

The word "function" here in Romans 12:4 is the Greek word *praxis*. The King James Version translates this word as "office,"— *all members have not the same office*. This suggests or implies an elevated title or position, which is unfortunate because it gives the word a skewed connotation to our ears. But when this Greek word *praxis* is used in Scripture, it's translated "works" or "deeds." It's translated "works" in Matthew 16:27 (KJV) where Jesus said:

Matthew 16:27

For the Son of man shall come in the glory of his Father with his angels; and then he shall reward every man according to his **works** (according to his **deeds**—NASB).

This truth brings out an important point—that many people are looking for a title, position or an office, but God wants them to be more concerned with just being faithful in *works* or *deeds*. The position comes later as the individual is faithful in the *works*. So Romans 12:4 is saying that we don't all have the same function, works or deeds, but we ALL have works and deeds we should be engaged in.

The motive for getting involved in church work, however, should not be "What can I get out of it?" The motive should be the desire to be obedient to God for the welfare of the whole and furtherance of His kingdom. Maturity is looking at the welfare of the church and saying, "What can I do to help?" President

John F. Kennedy put it this way, "Ask not what your country can do for you, but what you can do for your country." Shouldn't such an attitude exist all the more with Christians toward the kingdom of God? Involvement includes humility. It's not always going to be done *your way.* I have seen many people with the attitude, "Well, if I can't do this my way, forget it, let them do it without me." That kind of thinking is a sign of spiritual and emotional immaturity. The kingdom of God will be furthered when we all lay our lives down and strip ourselves of self-ambition so that we can all flow together as a team, as one body with each other. So make sure your motive for functioning in the local church is not to further your personal agenda, but to advance the kingdom of God.

Every believer is called by God to both fit and function in the local church. But the million-dollar question is...what are they supposed to be doing?

We have found that for Christians to be the most **fruitful** and **fulfilled**, they must have a match in three areas: **gift**, **passion**, **temperament** (or personal style). This comes from Bruce Bugbee's book, *What You Do Best in the Body of Christ: Discover Your Spiritual Gifts, Personal Style, and God-Given Passion*, Zondervan, 2005.

What: Spiritual Gifts

1 Corinthians 12:1

Now concerning spiritual gifts, brothers, **I do not want you to be uninformed.**

What's ironic about this verse is that most Christians are totally *uniformed* about spiritual gifts, and specifically, what their spiritual gifts are. And this verse is from the very same chapter about us being connected and functioning together as members of one body!

When you became a follower of Christ, God gave you some spiritual gifts that He expects you to be using for His glory.

Romans 12:6

Having gifts that differ according to the grace given to us, **let us use them.**

1 Peter 4:10

As **each has received a gift**, use it to serve one another, as good stewards of God's varied grace.

Now that you have a gift...use it to serve! The New American Standard Bible puts it this way:

As each one has received a special gift, **employ it** in serving one another as good stewards of the manifold grace of God

Employ that gift! The word "employ" means "put it to work." If everyone in the church served regularly using their spiritual gifts, the load on any one given individual or group would be much lighter, and the mission of the church would be accomplished with greater success.

Spiritual gifts are divine enablements. They are different from mere human talent, although sometimes they are connected. In Scripture, we have lists of these spiritual gifts. The Apostle Paul was a list-maker. He did this with the fruit of the Spirit, the works of the flesh and the adversities he experienced as he served God. But he also made lists of spiritual gifts.

Here is Paul's list along with gifts mentioned other places in Scripture (I've eliminated repetition in multiple lists):

1 Corinthians 12:8-10

1. The word of wisdom
2. The word of knowledge
3. Faith
4. Gifts of healing
5. The working of miracles
6. Prophecy
7. Discerning of spirits
8. Tongues
9. Interpretation of tongues

1 Corinthians 12:28

10. Apostle
11. Prophet
12. Teacher (+ Ephesians 4:11)
13. Helps (serving)
14. Administration

Ephesians 4:11

15. Evangelist/evangelism
16. Pastor-Shepherds

Romans 12:6-9

17. Teaching (+ 1 Peter 4:11)
18. Exhortation

19. Giving (generosity)
20. Leadership
21. Mercy

1 Peter 4:9-11

22. Hospitality

Exodus 31:3, Exodus 35:30-33

23. Craftsmanship

Psalm 150:3-5

24. Creative communication (singers, musicians, and today—technical and audio/visual gifts)

Some people would add intercession (1 Timothy 2:1-2, Romans 8:26-27), and celibacy (1 Corinthians 7:7).

As a believer and follower of Jesus Christ, God has given you spiritual gifts and expects you to use them in kingdom service. I believe you most likely have two or three top spiritual gifts that you should be focusing on. It's not the purview or scope of this book to teach on spiritual gifts, but for further study, consider reading:

What You Do Best in the Body of Christ - Bruce Bugbee - 2009 - Zondervan

S.H.A.P.E.: Finding and Fulfilling Your Unique Purpose for Life - Erik Rees - 2008 - Zondervan

Discover Your Spiritual Gifts: The Easy-to-Use Guide That Helps You Identify and Understand Your Unique God-Given Spiritual Gifts - C. Peter Wagner - 2012 - Chosen Books

You might also take a free online test to help you discover your gifts at: www.giftstest.com

But I want to emphasize, we're commanded by God to function in and with our spiritual gifts. It's not a suggestion.

Romans 12:6

> Having gifts that differ according to the grace given to us, **let us use them**.

Ain't My Gift—Not Doing That

One issue I've seen with some people after they learn about spiritual gifts, is the "ain't my gift, not doing that" problem. The extreme of this is when you see a paper towel on the floor of the church restroom and say to yourself, "The ministry of helps is not my gift, so...not picking it up." But what we need to understand is that any family has common household chores that everyone is expected to chip in and help with.

For example, little Buford may have a normal family chore of taking out the trash to the curb on Monday nights. This is Buford's gift and passion, he loves it. On the first Friday evening of April dad announces, "Well gang, tomorrow morning, before we get too far into our weekend, we're going to spend up until lunchtime doing spring cleaning around the yard, garage and house, so don't plan on going anywhere until we're finished." Little Buford protests, "I'm sorry Dad, but I won't be doing that. My chore is to take the trash out on Monday nights. But...glory to God, I'll be cheering the rest of you on!" Dad then has to explain to Bufford that there's this thing called 'common family chores' that the whole family helps with from time to time, and you're expected to help, gifted or not.

I've seen this kind of thing play out in the church. For some smaller churches that struggle to find nursery volunteers, they have a team of main volunteers that are scheduled for weekend services, but they expect mothers and fathers to volunteer once every month or two in order to have another adult present to do crowd control and potty patrol. What we've seen is, not being sensitive to common family responsibilities, they reply, "Oh, that's not my gift, sorry." But whether it's nursery and children's church, spring cleaning, or helping out at the huge outreach event, we all have family responsibilities that we should get involved with. Love for the church family should motivate us to do so.

Galatians 5:13

> For you were called to freedom, brothers. Only do not use your freedom as an opportunity for the flesh, but **through love serve one another**.

Where: Passion

Whereas ***Gift*** answers the "what" question, what you'll be doing; ***passion*** answers the "where" question, where you'll be serving. (*What You Do Best in the Body of Christ*, by Bruce Bugbee)

Passion is a strong desire, emotion and attraction to a specific cause or people-group that ignites energy and action. It's an area that fires you up and gets you excited. It's what would be the focus of your conversation when sitting around a campfire late into the night talking about God and His kingdom. It's sometimes felt as a burden or something burning within one's heart.

Passion is generally connected to a cause or people-group. Sometimes it's both a cause and a people-group. Nehemiah had a passion for a cause...to see the walls of Jerusalem rebuilt. Paul had passion for reaching Gentiles while Peter had passion for reaching the Jews. William Booth (1829-1912, founder of the Salvation Army) had a passion for reaching the poor and marginalized. Some people have a passion for reaching children and youth, some for reaching unwed mothers—all use their gifts in a place where they are energized and care deeply about the cause or people they are touching.

Psalm 37:4

> Delight yourself in the Lord, and he will give you the desires of your heart.

There are two ways to look at this verse.

1. ***Delight yourself in the Lord and He will give you the desires of your heart***, meaning, He will fulfill those desires and bring them to pass. I believe that's true.

2. ***Delight yourself in the Lord and He will give you the desires of your heart***, meaning, He will put those desires in your heart in the first place, those desires will be God-placed, God-given. I believe that's true as well.

What cause or people-group do you have a passion to see God do a work in: children, seniors, singles, new believers, men's ministry, women's ministry, youth, college-career age? What area of ministry fires you up: Worship, discipleship, leadership development, small groups, hospitality, evangelism, food pantry, facility and grounds, prayer ministry, community outreach, sports outreach, benevolence to those in need, administration and organization; helping with Sunday services in music, sound or technical gifts?

How: Temperament (Personal Style)

Gifts answer the "what" question, ***passion*** answers the "where" question, but temperament, what Bruce Bugee calls ***personal style***, answers the "how" question.

Personal style and temperament takes into account your unique hardwiring from God as far as personality. Some are extroverts, some are introverts. Some are task-oriented, some are people-oriented.

Placing an outgoing people-oriented person all by themselves in a small office doing computer work would not be the best fit. Conversely, putting a more quiet, introverted person greeting people at the front door would be a mismatch as well. We need to serve in a place that best fits how God made us.

Psalm 139:1, 13-14

> O Lord, you have searched me and known me! ... For you formed my inward parts; you knitted me together in my mother's womb. ... I praise you, for I am fearfully and wonderfully made.

Your basic personality type is God-given, and should be taken into account when deciding on a place to serve.

Where should you get involved? The best place to get involved in a church is a place where all three of these things (gift, passion, temperament) are aligned and flow together for maximum fruit-bearing. For help in this area, I encourage you to get the book mentioned above by Bruce Bugbee (*What You Do Best in the Body of Christ*), or the book by Erik Rees called, *S.H.A.P.E.: Finding and Fulfilling Your Unique Purpose for Life* (Zondervan - 2008).

The Church: A Spiritual Building

Earlier I mentioned that the church is a spiritual building.

Ephesians 2:21

> (Christ Jesus), in whom the whole structure, being joined together, grows into a holy temple in the Lord.

1 Peter 2:5

> You yourselves like living stones are being built up as a spiritual house.

You are a stone in God's spiritual house, the church. You are not only a stone in the universal church, you are a stone in the spiritual house of the local church. In the natural, if a stone in a foundation of a building is missing or out of place, two things result: the entire structure is weakened, and secondly, more pressure is placed on the stones surrounding the one missing or out of place. And this is exactly what happens when people don't function or get involved in the local church and choose to remain benchwarmers.

The presence of God dwelt in the Old Testament tabernacle just as the presence of God dwells in the midst of His Body, the Church. 1 Corinthians 3:16 from the Amplified Bible brings this out.

1 Corinthians 3:16

> Do you not know and understand that you [the church] are the temple of God, and that the Spirit of God dwells [permanently] in you [collectively and individually]? (AMP)

As the local church is a spiritual house made up of people fitting and functioning in their proper places, the Old Testament tabernacle can give us some insight into the makeup of the New Testament church. In Exodus 26, God gave Moses specific instructions on how to erect the tabernacle. There's one verse that caught my interest.

Exodus 26:17

> There shall be two tenons (NIV: projections) for each board, fitted to one another; thus you shall do **for all the boards of the tabernacle.** (NASB)

The Old Testament tabernacle is a type or shadow of the New Testament (spiritual) universal church along with the local church. Notice again in Exodus 26:17

there are to be two tenons or projections for each board in the building. When I first began this study, I had no idea what a tenon was. Then it talks about "sockets."

Exodus 26:19

> Two sockets under one board for its two tenons and two sockets under another board for its two tenons. (NASB)

What in the world is this talking about? After some investigation, I found out that a tenon was a projection of some kind, and a socket was the groove or hole that the tenon fit into. A tenon was either a peg that protruded or a tongue, like tongue and groove boards. Either way, the boards of the tabernacle were created with both a projection and socket. One board's projection would snugly fit into the hole or groove of the adjacent board.

This is a picture of what the local church is supposed to be like because it beautifully describes what was said in Ephesians 4:16, "joined and held together," or as Strong's Greek dictionary defined that phrase, "fitly framed together." Each board is fitly framed together with the board before and after it.

The Lord showed me something about the boards of the tabernacle, and by extension, the spiritual building of the church. Remember, each board had a projection (tongue or peg) and a socket (groove or hole). The projection represents something that extends from you...something you GIVE into someone else; a gift, talent or contribution that is used to bless someone else or the church. A groove or hole is a place to receive from others that are extending into your life; a need that must be supplied by someone else's gift, talent or contribution. Each person has both a tongue and a groove, something to give and something to receive. A person who always receives but never gives (supplying their gift) is a board without the projection or tongue, and such a board would cause the building to be unstable.

When each person in a local church is fitted and functioning, the church will be extremely strong and be able to bear a lot of pressure and weight that the devil will throw against it. I believe this principle of everyone fitting and functioning is one key (certainly not the only one) that helps churches to thrive.

Matthew 16:18

> On this rock I will build my church, and the gates of hell shall not prevail against it.

It is the key of unity, of being in one accord, of everyone doing their part. When this happens, the gates of hell will not overcome it. Everyone in unity doing their part is the key.

1 Corinthians 1:10

> I appeal to you, brothers, by the name of our Lord Jesus Christ, that all of you agree, and that there be no divisions among you, but that you be united in the same mind and the same judgment.

Once, in our church service, I demonstrated this principle of fitting and functioning by having 20 men from the congregation come up to the front. I placed 10 on one side and 10 on the other and gave them a rope for a tug of war. The catch was that, the last second before I said "Go!," I told those on the left to hold the rope and use all their strength, but told those on the right that only five of them were to grab on and pull. The other five were just to "be there and watch." The outcome was predictable with the 10-man "all hands on" side winning easily. This visually demonstrated to the congregation the principle of fit and function. Just being there not grabbing on and helping affects the whole team.

If everyone did his or her part, the church would be strong. It seems Satan can get the upper hand in a church easily when the majority are just spectators. Every ministry and department within the church would be so much better if everyone began to function in the right place with their gift-passion-temperament match. Praise and worship would be enhanced so much if everyone with musical talent and skill joined the group. This would be true for every department.

What We Carry into Eternity

What we do with our lives affects both the natural and the eternal. Our time, talent and treasure is helping to build something, but...not everything builds toward the eternal.

1 Corinthians 3:10-15

> Now if anyone builds on the foundation with gold, silver, precious stones, wood, hay, straw—each

> one's work will become manifest, for the Day will disclose it, because it will be revealed by fire, and the fire will test what sort of work each one has done. If the work that anyone has built on the foundation survives (is carried into eternity), he will receive a reward. If anyone's work is burned up, he will suffer loss, though he himself will be saved, but only as through fire.

The gold, silver, and precious stones will be left standing; but the wood, hay and straw will burn up. Everything but that which is eternal is going to burn up in the end. The building that you work in and everything in it is going to burn up. All your possessions and photos are going to burn up. At the end of the world, there will definitely be global warming, but the earth won't end because of your hairspray or cow farts, it's going to end with a roaring, blazing fire that destroys the entire earth.

2 Peter 3:10

> But the day of the Lord will come like a thief, and then the heavens will pass away with a roar, and the heavenly bodies will be burned up and dissolved, and the earth and the works that are done on it will be exposed.

Everything burns up in the end. Your hobbies, trophies, money, houses, cars, motorcycles, ATVs, snowmobiles, jet skis, airplanes, bowling balls, video games, movies, cottages, second homes, surf boards, beach umbrellas, jewelry, clothes...everything is burned up in the end. The only thing we carry into eternity is that which has contributed to the kingdom of God. What you're doing for XYZ Company, Inc. is commendable, but it won't last. I'm advocating for fitting and functioning in the church of our Lord Jesus Christ, the only thing on this earth that carries over into eternity.

It's interesting to note what the Apostle Paul said as he closed his letters to the churches. Here are some examples.

Romans 16

1 I commend to you our sister Phoebe, **a servant of the church** at Cenchreae.

3 Greet Prisca and Aquila, my **fellow workers** in Christ Jesus,

6 Greet Mary, who has **worked hard** for you.

7 Greet Andronicus and Junia, my kinsmen and my **fellow prisoners.**

9 Greet Urbanus, our **fellow worker** in Christ,

12 Greet those **workers in the Lord**, Tryphaena and Tryphosa. Greet the beloved Persis, who has **worked hard** in the Lord.

1 Corinthians 16:15-16

Now I urge you, brothers—you know that the household of Stephanas were the first converts in Achaia, and that they have **devoted themselves to**

the service of the saints— be subject to such as these, and to **every fellow worker and laborer.**

Colossians 4:7-11

7 He (Tychicus) is a beloved brother and **faithful helper** who **serves with me in the Lord's work.**

9 I am also sending Onesimus, a **faithful and beloved brother**, one of your own people. ...

10 Aristarchus, who is **in prison with me**, sends you his greetings...

11 These are the only Jewish believers among **my co-workers**; they **are working with me here for the Kingdom of God**. And what a comfort they have been! (NLT)

The people that had a special place in Paul's heart were the people who were in the trench with him serving. They were the ones who didn't sit back, but rolled up their sleeves and used their gifts and passions to serve the church and further God's kingdom. These people didn't just "fit," they "functioned."

Our last chapter—one of the most important, deals with our attitudes while fitting and functioning. Our attitude either makes us or breaks us. But there are some attitudes in our functioning that we must have in order for our efforts to be truly productive. So please don't skip the next chapter!

Only one life, twill soon be past,

Only what's done for Christ will last.

- C.T. Studd (English missionary, 1860-1931

Chapter 8

Functioning with Faithfulness

So there you have it: *Fit, Function, and Flourish.* These are the words that the Lord spoke to me that night, words that were so strong when spoken that they woke me up. And I believe the message was very clear: flourishing spiritually comes after you fit and function in the body, the church. To be clear, it's not the only key, but it's an important one.

I would like to end this book with some principles that you'll need in combination with what has already been said. It's possible to "fit and function" but with a wrong attitude. One principle that we need to understand is that flourishing and God's promotion come **after** faithfulness.

Proverbs 20:6

> Many a man proclaims his own steadfast love, but a faithful man who can find?

Proverbs 28:20

> A faithful man will abound with blessings.

Blessing comes after faithfulness. Many would like to bypass this principle and go directly into the promotion and blessing, but that's not how God works. "Promotion comes after faithfulness" is a principle that even God used when it came to His own Son!

Philippians 2:8, 9

> And being found in human form, he humbled himself by becoming obedient to the point of death, even death on a cross. Therefore (because He humbled Himself) God has highly exalted him and bestowed on him the name that is above every name,

Jesus was faithful in His ministry. He was obedient to go to the cross and that faithfulness resulted in God highly exalting Him. Promotion comes after faithfulness. This is a principle that not even the Son would bypass (nor did He want to).

A faithful man will abound with blessings. We see this principle in Paul's life.

1 Timothy 1:12

> I thank him who has given me strength, Christ Jesus our Lord, because he judged me faithful, appointing me to his service.

Paul did not start out as an apostle. He began by being faithful to learn from the Spirit of God the truths of Christianity and to witness to these truths at every opportunity. As he became faithful to learn and to do, God began to promote him. I have known of people who have wanted to quit their jobs and just start into the ministry. No, just be faithful in the church you are at now, and God will see to it that you are promoted. Joshua served Moses and got promoted by the Lord. Elisha served Elijah and was promoted. The disciples served Jesus and were promoted. Titus served Paul and later was promoted to pastor over Crete. Philip served tables in Acts 6 and, later, God promoted him to be an evangelist (Acts 21:8). Be faithful where you are with a good attitude, and God will promote you. Don't try to promote yourself! Do you remember the parable of the talents?

Matthew 25:21

> His master said to him, 'Well done, good and faithful servant. You **have been faithful** over a little; **I will set you over much**. Enter into the joy of your master.'

In this case and in this sense, your past determines your future. Promotion comes after faithfulness. In churches where I pastored, I didn't put people into higher positions of **authority** until they have proven themselves faithful in the lower positions of **responsibility**. If they had been faithful in the lower positions and kept a good attitude, then they could expect more. So many times, I have seen people trying to exalt themselves or their "own" ministries. When you are in a church, "your" ministry had better be part of and in line with the church's ministry! Self-ambition is one of the most dangerous attitudes prevalent in the church today. Self-ambition causes division, and there is no place for it in the Church.

In 2 Samuel 15:1-6, we see an example of self-ambition. This is the story of what is called the “sin of Absalom.” Absalom cut off the people who were going to David, so that he could make a name for himself. He told those seeking the king's help that David could not help them as much as he could. He then showed them friendliness and affection. We see the sin of Absalom in verse 6.

2 Samuel 15:6

> Thus Absalom did to all of Israel who came to the king for judgment. So Absalom stole the hearts of the men of Israel.

This is self-ambition, and you need to watch out for it. I have seen people who became very outgoing and friendly to other people in the congregation in order to develop their loyalty with dubious intent.

I have heard this said sometimes: "Hey, I'm not here to serve man. I'm here to serve only God." That sounds right, but is it?

Joshua 1:1

> Now it came about after the death of **Moses the servant of the Lord**, that the Lord spoke to **Joshua** the son of Nun, **Moses' servant**, saying... (NASB)

Look at this closely because we need to get hold of this concept. Moses was the servant of the Lord, but Joshua was the servant of Moses.

Joshua was Moses' right-hand man. Here is the principle in this: **By serving Moses, Joshua was serving**

the Lord! Because of Joshua's faithful attitude toward Moses, God promoted him. The fact is that you are serving your pastor and church, and there's nothing wrong with putting it that way. In serving your pastor and church by fitting and functioning, you are serving God. Just be faithful where you are, and God will promote you.

Some people always seem to want a teaching ministry in the church somewhere. Although that may be where God eventually calls a person, that's not the place you start. Be faithful, then promotion to other areas will be delegated to you.

2 Timothy 2:2:

> And what you have heard from me in the presence of many witnesses **entrust to faithful men**, who **will be able to teach others** also.

Faithfulness in some other area came first, then teaching. I have had people say to me, "Pastor Tom, I'm called to a pulpit ministry!' My response was, "You are? Are you willing to volunteer in another area for a few months first?" You see, you don't just start with a pulpit ministry or some position of leadership. Be faithful in the little things first, and let God promote you in His timing. As soon as you rush things, you are going to have problems.

Releasing Your Pastor

There is a beautiful story of Exodus 18:13-24 that talks about Moses getting exhausted because of burnout in the ministry. Jethro, Moses' father-in-law, told Moses that he needed to appoint helpers.

Exodus 18:18

> You and the people with you will certainly wear yourselves out, for the thing is too heavy for you. You are not able to do it alone.

Verses 21-22 gave the solution:

> Moreover, look for able men from all the people, men who fear God, who are trustworthy and hate a bribe, and place such men over the people as chiefs of thousands, of hundreds, of fifties, and of tens. And let them judge the people at all times.

Moses heeded the advice from his father-in-law and appointed men to help him judge. This freed or released Moses for more of the ministry to which he was called. Most pastors wear out, or "burnout;' because their congregations—by their lack of supplying their parts, have forced their pastors and church leaders to do too much. When that happens, the church leaders spend less time in the Word and prayer, and their own ministry to the people suffers.

The same principle we saw in Exodus 18 with Moses is seen in the book of Acts with the Apostles.

Acts 6:1-7

> [1] Now in these days when the disciples were increasing in number, a complaint by the Hellenists

arose against the Hebrews because their widows were being neglected in the daily distribution.

[2] And the twelve summoned the full number of the disciples and said, "It is not right that we should give up preaching the word of God to serve tables.

[3] Therefore, brothers, pick out from among you seven men of good repute, full of the Spirit and of wisdom, whom we'll appoint to this duty (delegation).

[4] But we'll devote ourselves to prayer and to the ministry of the word."

[5] And what they said pleased the whole gathering, and they chose Stephen, a man full of faith and of the Holy Spirit, and Philip, and Prochorus, and Nicanor, and Timon, and Parmenas, and Nicolaus, a proselyte of Antioch.

[6] These they set before the apostles, and they prayed and laid their hands on them.

[7] And the word of God continued to increase, and the number of the disciples multiplied greatly in Jerusalem, and a great many of the priests became obedient to the faith.

When the people of the church got involved and functioned, supplying their part, the apostles were released to get into the Word and prayer and church growth was the result. This is exactly what Ephesians 4:16 said...if everyone will supply their part and get involved with working and serving, the Body will grow.

If we'll do it God's way, it will work. Acts 6 is the story of the ministry of helps in action.

The Time to Start Is Now

Ecclesiastes 9:10 says:

> Whatever your hand finds to do, do it with your might.

The time to start fitting and functioning in a local church is now. Don't wait for some super-spiritual experience with goose bumps to come all over you as a sign from God that you are to start. This is His Word, and He wants you to flow with His revealed will. Someone once defined success as "finding a need and filling it." That's pretty good. We understand, of course, that to have maximum productivity, we want to find the right people for the right ministries or jobs. We don't want to put square pegs in round holes. Yet, at the same time, we have this Ecclesiastes 9:10 principle, *Whatever your hand finds to do, do it with your might.*

The balance to these two ideas is that if you will go ahead and find a need, fill it, and be faithful in it, God will promote you to something that more suits your gift.

Proverbs 18:16 says:

> A man's gift makes room for him and brings him before the great.

Be faithful, and God will promote you to where you fit best. Don't wait to start out where you fit best. You may wait forever!

For the first eight years of my Christian life, I grew up with what some of us call "**the red light principle**." This principle states that you should never do anything until the Holy Spirit descends on you with overwhelming power and, and with a thundering loud voice, commissions you to do something. The assumption here is that you have a red light from God, so keep the vehicle of your life on hold until you see some cosmic green light. Then, and only then, do you dare move out to do something for God. After all, we dare not sin by getting in the flesh! Some people are so afraid of moving in the flesh that they never do end up moving in the Spirit. But I have never known God to get angry because one of His children volunteered to serve in the church in some capacity.

Jesus said, in Matthew 28:19 "Go." That's a green light. Since learning some things, I now go by the "**green light principle**." The green light principle states that you should assume that you have a green light and go ahead and get your vehicle in motion. Once your vehicle is in motion, if you find out that it's the wrong direction, don't worry, God will show you by giving you a red light, and you can change direction. But assume initially that you have the green light.

Have you ever tried turning the steering wheel of a car when it's stopped? It's very hard. But, once you get that vehicle in motion, it's very easy to turn that wheel. It's the same thing with our lives. If you're doing nothing, it's very hard for God to steer your life and give you direction. But, if you'll operate by faith, step on out and do whatever your hand finds to do, then God can more readily direct you. We see this in the life of Paul in Acts 16.

Acts 16:7-10

And when they **had come** up to Mysia, they **attempted to go** into Bithynia, but the Spirit of Jesus did not allow them. So, **passing by** Mysia, **they went down to** Troas. And a vision appeared to Paul in the night: a man of Macedonia was standing there, urging him and saying, "Come over to Macedonia and help us." And when Paul had seen the vision**, immediately we sought to go** on into Macedonia, concluding that God had called us to preach the gospel to them.

Notice, in these verses, the verbs of action: *came up to - attempted to go into - passing by - went down to - we sought to go on into.* All these phrases speak of action, of going and doing something. God gave direction to Paul only after Paul was in motion. **Paul assumed he had the green light** to go to Bithynia and, on the way there, God gave him a red light. Don't wait around for something to do. There is plenty to do. If you don't know what to do, go ask your pastor or other church leader, and let them direct you to what needs to be done.

I've been to Israel five times. One of the things that intrigued me while there was the difference between the Sea of Galilee and the Dead Sea. The Sea of Galilee is called the Sea of Life because it receives water from the mountains in the north (Mount Hermon) and gives off the water it receives to the Jordan River to flow south. It receives and then gives, on a constant basis, and that is what gives it life. The water then flows south in the Jordan River to the Dead Sea. Unlike the

Sea of Galilee, the Dead Sea receives but never gives out. The Dead Sea is exactly that— dead! There is not one living thing in the Dead Sea, not one fish, not one organism, nothing. It receives but never gives out. Dead, dead, dead. God's plan for nature, and for you, is to receive and then give out.

Jesus told His disciples in Matthew 10:8, *freely you received, freely give.* When you contribute your part to the local church and function there with faithfulness, you are unleashing the law of life and blessing into your life. Again, *A faithful man will abound with blessings* (Proverbs 28:20).

As I have said, the time to start is now. Perhaps I should put it this way: only start when you would like God to start blessing you! Someone will say, "What you're saying doesn't line up. I know someone who isn't involved with a church at all, and they seem happy and make $300,000 a year. They have everything they want. They take five exotic vacations a year. What about them?"

Just because someone is blessed financially or materially doesn't mean they are flourishing in the other areas of life. Money is only one small part of flourishing. You can have all the money in the world, but that is not going to heal your marriage, heal your body or set you free from depression or lust. Don't be fooled by someone who is not involved or functioning in a church, yet has a lot of money. This is easily proved in Scripture. Listen to Jesus' words to the lukewarm church at Laodicea.

Revelation 3:16-18

> So, because **you are lukewarm**, and neither hot nor cold, I will spit you out of my mouth. For **you say, I am rich, I have prospered, and I need nothing, not realizing that you are wretched, pitiable, poor, blind, and naked.** I counsel you to buy from me gold refined by fire, so that you may be rich, and white garments so that you may clothe yourself and the shame of your nakedness may not be seen, and salve to anoint your eyes, so that you may see.

The people Jesus was talking to in these verses thought they were rich, but they really weren't, not spiritually anyhow. What was their sin? Verse 16 gives us the key: *So because you are lukewarm, and neither hot nor cold, I will spit you out of My mouth.* The problem was that they were lukewarm. They were rich in the natural but weren't hot for God and His kingdom. Don't be fooled by this. Flourishing is much more than just financial.

A Right Heart

God is interested in your attitude while you are fitting and functioning. Your attitude needs to be one of proper motives. God wants you to function with faithfulness. Acts 8 is the story of Philip's great success in Samaria. People were getting saved and baptized and, later in the chapter, Peter and John came down from Jerusalem to pray that they be filled with the Holy Spirit. Simon the Sorcerer wanted to get in on this ability to lay his hands on people and have them filled with the Spirit. We know from verses 18 and 22 that his motives and attitude were not right. Notice what Peter said in verse 21.

Acts 8:21

> You have neither part nor lot in this matter, **for your heart is not right before God.**

This gives us some insight into the attitude that God desires for those who want to get involved in ministry: that your heart be right! Simon's heart wasn't right and that excluded him from the ministry there, and Peter saw right through it. Sometimes people's hearts aren't right, and they're doing something for their ego or their own ends. Sometimes you see it with singers and musicians who perform in such a way so as to draw attention to themselves. But they need to be instructed that it's not about drawing attention to themselves, it's about drawing people's attention to Jesus. Here's a formula that I've tried to use with people serving:

Ability + Attitude = Authority.

It simply means that a person must have not only the ability to do a certain function but also a good attitude before they should be given any authority. I love it when people seek *responsibility*, but when I sense people are after *authority*, red flags go up in my mind. And there is a difference between **you rising up** and **God raising you up**. In Numbers 16:2 we read about

Korah and gang rising up. It didn't go well with them, the earth opened up and swallowed them and their families (verse 32). Compare that to Joshua 1 when God is the one who legitimately raised Joshua up. Big difference.

I have known many people who had tremendous abilities in areas that our church really needed. But, as much as I could have used their talents, I couldn't release them to function because they just didn't have the right attitude, it was all about them.

God uses people who have a cooperative spirit, free from self-ambition. Additionally, people need to get free from a spirit of criticism. A critical or independent spirit has caused more harm in churches than anything else I know. The church in the book of Acts grew because they were in one accord. When the people of the church fit and function with an attitude of faithfulness, both they and their local churches will flourish and grow as they touch and transform their communities.

My prayer for you is that you will take to heart the principles covered in this book and act on them. Attending and being involved in a local church is not a panacea for all your problems. I do believe, however, that it's an essential part of God's overall plan to be able to bless you. These three elements: *fit*, *function*, *and flourish*, are a God-given plan for your life. If obeyed with a faithful attitude, these principles will change your life. Let's come together and get to work.

Romans 12:6

Having gifts that differ according to the grace given to us, **let us use them.**

About the Author

Tom Peers has been in ministry since 1979. He grew up in Brockport, New York; attended Monroe Community College, Rochester, New York; State University of New York at Brockport, served in the United States Air Force and Air National Guard, graduated from Rhema Bible College in Broken Arrow, Oklahoma, and attended Elim Bible Institute, Lima, New York.

Tom has served as a pastor in Rochester, New York; Lake Worth, Florida; Florence, Kentucky; Cumberland, Maine and Portsmouth, New Hampshire; along with serving as Director of Operations for a Christian ministry in Phoenix, Arizona. He has also served fulltime as a certified church consultant. Tom and his wife Debby have two children, Jesse and Carissa, each with families of their own. Tom and Debby currently reside in Portland, Maine.

tompeers53@gmail.com

Books by Tom Peers:

The Pastor and the Prayer
Addiction Recovery Through Living the Serenity Prayer

Lord and Savior
A Savior to be Received From - A Lord to be Obeyed

Fit, Function and Flourish
Your Place and Function in the Local Church

Is God to Blame?
Reconciling Suffering with a Good God

How to Be a Prime Target
We're All Targets - Some Make Better Targets Than Others

Mixed Nuts
Brain Droppings From a Retired Pastor

www.ingramcontent.com/pod-product-compliance
Lightning Source LLC
Chambersburg PA
CBHW020503030426
42337CB00011B/220
* 9 7 8 0 9 9 7 0 9 9 8 2 9 *